ACCOUNTING CLASSICS SERIES

Publication of this Classic was made possible

by a grant from Arthur Andersen & Co.

Suggestions of titles to be included
in the Series are solicited and should
be addressed to the Editor.

Accounting Publications of Scholars Book Co.

ROBERT R. STERLING, EDITOR

CENTRALIZATION VS. DECENTRALIZATION IN
ORGANIZING THE CONTROLLER'S DEPARTMENT

A Research Study and Report

Prepared for

CONTROLLERSHIP FOUNDATION, INC.

by

HERBERT A. SIMON   GEORGE KOZMETSKY

HAROLD GUETZKOW   GORDON TYNDALL

of the

GRADUATE SCHOOL
OF INDUSTRIAL ADMINISTRATION

CARNEGIE INSTITUTE OF TECHNOLOGY

Scholars Book Co.
4431 Mt. Vernon
Houston, Texas 77006

197039

Reprinted 1978 Scholars Book Co.
with special permission of Financial Executives Research Foundation

Library of Congress Cataloging in Publication Data
Main entry under title:
Centralization vs. decentralization in organizing
  the controller's department.
  (Accounting classics series)
  Reprint of the ed. published by Controllership
Foundation, New York.
  1. Controllership. I. Simon, Herbert Alexander,
1916–   II. Financial Executives Research
Foundation, New York. III. Carnegie Institute of
Technology, Pittsburgh. Graduate School of
Industrial Administration.
HF5550.C333   1978   658.4   77-90343
ISBN 0-914348-24-8

Manufactured in the United States of America

PREFACE

Organizing is one of the central and inescapable tasks of top management. And the experienced executive is painfully aware of how little is known as to what constitutes effective organization. He sees around him, in other companies the same size as his and even engaged in the same line of business, a bewildering variety of solutions to organization problems. He has heard, on many occasions, inconclusive debates on the comparative merits of existing organization structures and proposed new ones.

The executive is conscious also of the wide gap that sometimes appears between rulebook and practice. He knows that organization is something more than charts and manuals — that what really counts is what people do and how they work together. His experience has taught him that to change an organization — the actual working relationships — involves a great deal more than issuing orders. In many cases he has acquired a real skepticism as to what can be accomplished by formal reorganization. Yet he knows too that formal organization is necessary in a large, complex enterprise. Making an organization work effectively involves more than just "getting the right men and putting them to work." Conscious thought and careful planning are required to bring these men together in an effective pattern of operation.

Because it has seen executives facing these issues in so many business concerns, even those that are most successful, the Graduate School of Industrial Administration regards the area of business organization as a major focus of its research. The goal is to broaden and deepen our understanding of human behavior in organizations, and to apply this understanding to the problem of organizing business enterprises. This goal rests on no illusion that a "science of organization" will replace experienced judgment in dealing with the specific organizational problems of specific companies. Rather, the aim of such a program must be to bring about the same kind of mutual support between "science" and "art" that has made possible the spectacular progress we have seen in technology over the past half century — the automobile, electric power and electronics, atomic energy. These have rested on a combination of patient research, developing basic scientific knowledge, and application of this knowledge to the solution of practical problems. This kind of interacting research — thus far rare in the management area — is the School's goal.

This attitude also motivates Controllership Foundation in setting as its objective the improvement of business management through better controllership. Hence it is natural that the two organizations should collaborate in this work. The organization study reported in this volume is an outgrowth of discussion between faculty members of the School and the staff of Controllership Foundation. The Foundation's trustees recognized that company controllers consider the centralization and

iii

decentralization of the controller's department in multi-plant firms an important and difficult organization problem. Accordingly, the Foundation agreed to provide funds for a study that would attempt to cast light on this problem through fundamental research. This study has been supported primarily by the Foundation's substantial grant, supplemented by additional funds provided by the School. Emerging as it has from an important practical question suggested by business executives, the study should provide at least a first test of the assumption of both organizations that fundamental research can be a helpful associate to the art of business management.

Readers accustomed to the standard literature on business organization may be surprised to find the major focus on informal day-to-day relationships between controllers and operating officials, on the types of communication and the lack of communication between different individuals in organizations, on the actual work activities of individuals in controllers' departments under varying degrees of decentralization. This focus, rather than the more common emphasis on formal line-and-staff relationships, is intentional, because a major goal of this study was to investigate what are the actual, informal, sometimes off-the-record relationships that prevail in business organizations under different degrees of centralization in different types of concerns.

Sometimes these informal relationships correspond to the formal organization charts; sometimes they do not. Sometimes decisions are in fact made by line officials on the data provided by the controller's staff; sometimes they are not. We need to know a great deal more about *why* informal decision-making procedures spring up outside formal organizational patterns, about why individuals sometimes behave quite differently from the way the organization chart instructs them. Only by understanding better the reasons why such behavior patterns emerge can we begin to predict what kinds of organizational arrangements will work best and under what conditions.

The research staff has written its findings as a report to company controllers. But in reading the report, I have reached the conclusion that it deserves the careful attention not only of controllers but of other executives as well. There are two reasons for this. First, the problems of the controller's department are largely problems of its relations with the other departments of the business. They can be solved by the controller only in cooperation with the other executives concerned. Second, questions of centralization and decentralization are not peculiar to the controller's department, but pervade the whole structure of modern business. While the field research was focused on controllers' departments, most of the findings of the report have an important bearing on the centralization-decentralization problem, in whatever department it is found.

I share the authors' hope that the results will be useful and stimulating in dealing with the organization of the controller's department, and in application to other organization problems that involve issues of centralization and decentralization.

G. L. BACH, *Dean*
Graduate School
   of Industrial Administration
Carnegie Institute of Technology

FOREWORD

The work of our modern industrial society is done through organizations — business concerns, universities, government agencies. How to organize effectively to accomplish our tasks becomes a central question in the application of social science knowledge to practical problems.

This study was undertaken to expand our knowledge about human behavior in organizations, and to do this in a way that would cast light on the specific problems of organizing effectively the controller's department in large companies. This report is a summary of findings and conclusions with respect to organization of the controllership function. It is directed to those executives in top management — both inside and outside controller's departments — who have the responsibility for bringing about a sound relationship between the controllership function and the other business functions that the controller's department serves.

The authors hope their conclusions will be found useful in companies that are faced with problems of centralization and decentralization. They hope, also, that over and above its specific organizational recommendations, the report will suggest a useable approach to questions of organization — an approach that can be applied by company executives in thinking through their own organizational problems. For this reason we have tried to set forth with some care not only our conclusions but also the way in which we arrived at them.

Study Procedure

To avoid burdening the body of this report with detail, we should like to summarize here:

1. The criteria that were used to evaluate the effectiveness of organizations.

2. The method that was used to obtain data from the seven companies that were surveyed.

What Is "Good" Organization?

The plan of this study was to observe controllers' departments of a number of companies in order to observe what kinds of organizational arrangements are effective. Before this could be done, we had to find answers to two difficult questions:

1. What do we mean by effective? What are the goals at which the activities of the controller's department are aimed?

2. How do we *observe and test* whether an organization is effective? What kinds of evidence will tell us how far a controller's department is succeeding in accomplishing its goals?

Ideally, in a business concern one would want to relate the organizational structure to profit: "How much greater would the profit be if we used this organizational plan rather than another?" There are several reasons why the question cannot be approached in this direct fashion. Out of the whole mass of factors that determine the profitability of a business enterprise, organization structure is only one — and not always a preponderant one. To try to measure directly the effect of organization on profit would be like trying to measure the effect of a Minnesota spring shower on the flow of water over Niagara Falls.

If we could "hold all other factors constant," this difficulty could, of course, be removed. But other factors cannot be held constant. No two companies are even approximately comparable. A before-and-after comparison of organizations would be beclouded by the effects of all the other trends in business conditions and company practice that were moving at the same time.

Therefore, the method of appraisal adopted was based on certain assumptions about the causal chain. The first assumption was that the controller's department contributes to profits through the informational services it provides to management and stockholders. Hence, we reason that if we could trace the effects of organizational structure upon these services, it would be justifiable to assume that the services, in turn, would be reflected sooner or later in the better accomplishment of company goals.

The second assumption was that the controller's department itself represents a direct drain on profits through the actual cost of departmental operation. Hence, if the same controllership service could be provided at a lower cost through one organizational structure than through another, the former was preferable.

The third assumption was that there are important long-range interactions between organization structure and the quality of the people operating the organization. Regardless of the immediate effectiveness of an organization, it would be short-sighted to appraise it without taking account of whether the kinds of experience it provided to the people in it tended to develop, or to hinder the development of, their abilities.

These three assumptions were used in answering the question of what we mean by effective organization of the controller's department. To be effective, the controller's department should:

> Provide informational services of high quality.
> Perform these services at a minimum cost.
> Facilitate the long-range development of competent accounting and operating executives.

But how can we actually observe how well a controller's department is achieving these goals? One of them, the *informational services,* we tried to observe directly by comparing the impact of controllership services on the behavior and decisions of operating executives in the various companies studied. Evidence with respect to the other two objectives was less direct. On *economy,* we attempted to estimate what differences there would be in the staff required to operate the controller's department under different organizational arrangements. Further, when we found that organizational changes had recently been made, we sought for evidence of the effects of these changes on accounting costs. On *personnel development,* we had to form some picture of the kinds of training and experience to which members of the organization would be exposed in the normal course of their careers under different plans of organization.

With these assumptions in mind, the framework of the study took shape:

1. Arrangements were made with seven companies to study their controller's departments. These companies were not intended to be, in any sense, a "random" sample. We were interested in large multi-location companies where problems of centralization and decentralization would be prominent. We wanted to include some that were regarded as relatively centralized, others that were thought to have gone rather far in the direction of decentralization. We wanted a sufficient range of industries, and types of industry to protect us in some measure against the danger of unwarranted generalization. The aim was not to sample American industry, but to get a sufficiently wide range of variation in the factors we were interested in studying.

2. The data for the study were obtained primarily from interviews with controllers, accounting and operating executives in the seven companies. The interview data were supplemented by the study of the actual accounting reports, and to a limited extent by observations of company personnel in the course of their daily activities. In all, more than 400 executives were interviewed. More than half of these were operating executives in manufacturing, sales, and other departments; the remainder were accounting executives. In position, they ranged from company presidents to supervisors of accounting sections, on the accounting side, and district sales managers and factory general foremen on the operating side. For special purposes, a few interviews were held with factory production clerks and with shift foremen.

3. The interviews were aimed at learning how the controllership service actually operated, and *not* whether the persons interviewed thought the organization structure was good or bad. If we could merely have asked executives which organizational arrangements worked well, and which badly, and recorded the answers, the whole study would have been simple. But our task was not to record existing *beliefs* about organization structure. Rather, it was to assist management by developing *new* evidence that would not ordinarily be available to the executive from his own organizational experience. Unless we could add substantially to the existing body of experience and knowledge, it would be hard to justify the heavy research investment.

4. The interviews did not follow a rigid schedule. In general, they lasted from an hour to three hours. The interviewers kept in mind a broad list of questions to which answers were needed. These questions fall under five general headings:

  a. The present organization of the controller's department, and the scope of controllership functions.
  b. The structure and content of the periodic accounting reports; the kinds of special reports prepared; the report flow in preparation and distribution.
  c. The channels used for communication among persons in the controller's department, and between the controller's and operating departments (including both oral and written communication); importance and frequency of use of each channel.

vii

d. The use made by operating executives of the periodic accounting reports, as viewed by both accounting and operating personnel; how they were used; and how often they were used.

e. Examples of operating decisions in which accounting information might be relevant; the levels and locations in the organization where such decisions are made; the actual role of the controller's department and of accounting information in the initiation of problem investigations and in the actual analyses.

In concluding this description of how we went about the study, it is only fair to call precautionary attention to some of its characteristics. There are two, in particular, usually a part of adequate research on problems of this type, which should be kept in mind.

First, much of the information obtained by observing and describing organizations is qualitative rather than quantitative, and therefore somewhat subjective. We might have counted and measured more than we did. We consciously chose the other course because we felt that the loss in precision and the dangers of biased observations were more than balanced by the advantages of preserving the richness and reality of the organizational situations.

Second, the study adopts a "cross-section" rather than a "time-trend" approach. We studied seven companies at a single point in time, rather than one or more companies over a long period. We made some use of past history and trends in these companies, but comparable data and qualitative analyses for earlier periods were, of course, not available. As much as possible, however, we tried to take account of this problem.

Acknowledgements

The debts of the authors for assistance in conducting the study are great and numerous. This research project was largely financed by a sizable grant from Controllership Foundation. This was supplemented by research funds of the Graduate School of Industrial Administration. Since successful marriages of sound fundamental research and practical application are still all too rare in social science, we were especially fortunate in the Foundation's enthusiastic support for a broad research plan. The research programs of the Foundation and the Graduate School rest on the premise that research is not practical, in any real sense of the word, unless it is fundamental and thorough. We found full sympathy in the Foundation for this "bedrock" approach.

The members of the Project Advisory Panel appointed by the Pittsburgh Control of the Controllers Institute of America have given many hours to guiding and advising the study from its initial planning stages through the preparation of the final report. Through them we have had access to a wealth of professional knowledge and experience of the controllership function. Our discussions with them, and their comments and suggestions, have been most helpful. The Advisory Panel members are listed on a previous page.

Seven companies opened their doors and their files to us, to permit us to gather the information for this study. We are grateful for the very cordial welcome given, and for the many man-hours of executive time — probably 1,000 in all — they contributed in interviews. These companies and their controllers are:

American Steel & Wire Division, U. S. Steel Company — Russell M. Braund
General Mills, Inc. — Gordon C. Ballhorn
Eastman Kodak Co. — C. J. Van Niel
H. J. Heinz Company — Frank B. Cliffe
National Supply Company — E. H. Thorsteinson
National Tube Division, U. S. Steel Company — Leo C. Simmons
Westinghouse Electric Corporation — Charles E. Headlee

Space does not permit us to thank individually the four hundred or more persons we interviewed, or the many who commented on earlier drafts of the manuscript. In addition to the company controllers, we should like to mention Mr. Hugh Phillips, Organization Planning Supervisor of the U. S. Steel Company, who was responsible for arranging the study within the two divisions of that company.

Full responsibility for the conclusions of the study and for this report is assumed by the senior research staff. Neither the Advisory Panel nor the companies studied were asked to place their approval on our conclusions. While they have undoubtedly helped us avoid many errors, we assume responsibility for the mistakes we have made and the conclusions we have reached. Thanks to Controllership Foundation's policy and practice, we have had full freedom to report what we saw — or thought we saw.

Four graduate assistants, whose names are listed above, served as able and devoted members of the research team. They conducted a large number of interviews and participated in the analysis of the interview data. We are indebted to them for many important and helpful ideas, both during the conduct of the study and in the review of the manuscript.

During the planning stages of the study, the research staff worked as a group. Mr. Kozmetsky took administrative responsibility for organizing the field work and the data analysis. The interviews were conducted by the research staff and the graduate assistants. The project director took primary responsibility for the initial draft of this report, but the final report is in every sense a joint product of the four members of the research staff.

HERBERT A. SIMON
Project Director

TABLE OF CONTENTS

Chapter 3

THE USE OF FIGURES BY MANAGEMENT

Chapter 4

ORGANIZATION FOR CONTROLLERSHIP SERVICE: CENTRALIZATION, DECENTRALIZATION

Chapter 5

ORGANIZING ACCOUNTING FOR FACTORIES AND SALES FUNCTIONS

Chapter 6

THE DEVELOPMENT OF ACCOUNTING PERSONNEL

Chapter 1

A SUMMARIZATION OF THIS REPORT

This is a study of the organization of the controller's department in large companies with geographically dispersed operations. It is aimed at the question of how far decentralization should be carried in the controller's department. Because one basic function of the controller's department is to be a "service" department to the rest of the business, the study is concerned with the internal organization of the department, and also with the relation between decentralization of this department and the organization of other departments.

In this summary chapter, the findings of the study will be presented in an abbreviated and relatively unqualified manner. Quotation out of context, even by the authors, can be misleading. For this reason, part of the chapter is devoted to a description of research methods used. Specific references are given at various nodal points of the summary to those parts of the succeeding chapters where a fuller discussion of the findings can be found.

WHAT IS "GOOD" ORGANIZATION? [1]

The study seeks to determine the *effectiveness* of different forms of departmental organization. Ideally, in a business concern the test of effectiveness is profit. But for testing the effectiveness of organizing the controller's department, the question cannot be approached in this direct fashion. Intra- and interdepartmental relations are too indirect and complex to be traced directly to profits. Hence, three indirect measures of effectiveness were used. A controller's department is effective to the extent that it —

Provides informational services of high quality.
Performs these services at a minimum cost.
Facilitates the long-range development of competent accounting and operating executives.

THE MEANING OF "CENTRALIZATION" AND "DECENTRALIZATION" [2]

The words "centralization" and "decentralization" are used with a wide variety of meanings. One of these meanings, however, is fundamental to the others, and it becomes the strategically important one for this study:

An administrative organization is centralized to the extent that decisions are made at relatively high levels in the organization; decentralized to the extent that discretion and authority to make important decisions are delegated by top management to lower levels of executive authority.

[1] This section is elaborated in the Foreword.
[2] This section summarizes the major findings of Chapter 2, pp. 13-21.

1

For example, a measure of the degree of centralization or decentralization in the whole production department would be obtained by observing the relative rôles of the vice president for manufacturing, the factory manager, and the factory department head, respectively, in important production decisions. The greater the part of company top level executives in decision-making, the greater the centralization of organization; the greater the rôle of factory executives, or factory department executives, the greater the decentralization in organization to the factory or factory department levels.

Survey observations indicate that these controllers' departments enter the decision-making process primarily as suppliers and analyzers of information, and as consultants. Therefore, "centralization" and "decentralization" in the controllers' departments must be related to the levels in other departments to which such information, and analytical and consulting services are supplied.

The relative degree of centralization or decentralization of the controller's department depends on at least five factors:

1. *The structure of the accounts and reports.* A decentralized account structure is one that provides a maximum of information about individual subordinate organization units (for example, individual factory departments, or sales districts), by means of separate cost statements or profit and loss statements for individual units.[3]

2. *The geographical location of accounting functions.* Geographical decentralization means locating the personnel of the controller's department in the company's factories and district offices rather than largely at the home office.

3. *Formal authority relations.* Decentralization of formal authority means attaching accounting units directly to the operating units whose activities they are recording — for example, placing the factory controller under the authority of the factory manager.

4. *Loyalties.* Decentralization of loyalties means encouraging accounting personnel to regard themselves as members of the operating "team" to which they are providing service.

5. *Channels of communication.* Decentralization of communication means building up direct contact and communication between accounting personnel and the executives and supervisors of decentralized operating units — for example, direct communication between the factory accounting department and factory department heads or personnel.

This study showed rather conclusively that the same degree of centralization and decentralization is not desirable with respect to all five of these factors.

MANAGEMENT'S USE OF FIGURES [4]

In the seven companies studied, accounting information is used at various executive levels to answer three different kinds of questions:

---

[3] Decentralization, in this sense, is a function of the amount of detailed information supplied about individual organization units. The form in which this information is to be provided (*e.g.*, the chart of accounts) will, of course, be determined primarily at top levels of the controller's department.

[4] This section summarizes the major findings of Chapter 3, pp. 22-39.

Score-card questions: "Am I doing well or badly?"
Attention-directing questions: "What problems should I look into?"
Problem-solving questions: "Of the several ways of doing the job, which is the best?"

The organizational problems of providing effective service to management in the score-card and attention-directing areas were usually quite different from those of providing services in the area of special studies. Different sets of operating executives are generally involved in the two areas; and the kinds of data and analyses used may be quite different. Because of these differences, a controller's department which is well organized to provide the one type of service, may or may not be well organized to provide the other.

Score-Card and Attention-Directing Uses

In a factory the total departmental variance from standard or from budget would be an example of an item of score-card significance and use for the supervisor of the department concerned.

To the factory manager, the cost variances of individual departments would be attention-directing items — they would be one of the pieces of information which would direct his attention to departments requiring more careful review.

Acceptance of standards and the constructive use of accounting data for score-card and attention-directing purposes requires that the operating executives have confidence in the standards and in the performance reports that go to their superiors. In all cases, a close and direct relationship between accounting personnel and operating personnel appeared to be the most important factor in producing this confidence. This relationship needed to be close in the standards-setting procedure so that the operating man might have an opportunity to negotiate a standard which he could regard as a reasonable and attainable forecast of his operations. The relationship needed to be close in the reporting process so that the operating man might have help in interpreting his variances, and might have a part in developing the explanations of off-standard performance that were presented to his superior. Hence, for effective attention-directing service, *it is essential for the controller's department to develop direct and active channels of communication with the operating executives at those points in the organization where operations are being measured.*

Problem-Solving Uses

When data are used for problem-solving purposes — to choose among alternative processes, to decide whether to buy new equipment, to help in policy decisions — a special study is usually required. This commonly draws upon engineering estimates and industrial engineering standards as well as accounting information and usually means going back into the basic records of the accounting system.

There are two principal ways in which accounting data may come into the problem-solving process:

3

Executives may turn to the regular accounting and statistical reports for help.

The controller's department may make special studies for particular problems.

In which of these directions does the greatest promise lie for improving this aspect of controllership service? In the direction of more elaborate periodic reports or in strengthening the special studies services? This study indicates that *further development of staff and facilities for special studies is a more promising direction of progress than elaboration of periodic accounting reports.*

CENTRALIZATION AND DECENTRALIZATION OF THE ACCOUNT STRUCTURE [5]

Two rather different kinds of decentralization are possible. One, which is sometimes called "responsibility accounting," consists in classifying actual and standard (or budgeted) costs according to the organizational unit primarily responsible for incurring the cost, and presenting periodic cost statements for each such unit. The other, sometimes described as "profit and loss accounting," consists essentially in treating interdepartmental and interdivisional transfers of manufactured and partially manufactured goods as "sales," thereby arriving at a profit and loss statement for individual organizational units like divisions, factories, sales districts, and sales branches.

Survey findings leave little doubt that *a decentralized account structure of one or the other of these two forms is desirable — at least down to the level of factory departments, sales districts, and individual sales branches.* A more difficult question is whether the decentralization should be in the direction of responsibility statements or profit and loss statements.

Where a company is divided into a number of relatively self-contained parts, each responsible for manufacturing and selling a group of products, profit and loss statements for these individual parts appear to be meaningful and effective. Decentralized profit and loss accounting runs into real difficulties when the parts of the company to which it is applied are not really self-contained — for example, when separate decentralized statements are prepared for manufacturing and for sales of the same products.

There are four main reasons for avoiding overelaboration of decentralized accounting reports: a) Reporting items not controllable at the respective decentralized units is an unnecessary expense; b) it decreases understanding of the reports, and discourages operating men from using them; c) it may lead to resentment; and d) it often causes tardiness in issuance of the accounting reports.

No evidence was found that decentralized profit and loss statements are more effective than decentralized responsibility statements in promoting profit consciousness. It is suggested that profit consciousness is best promoted along two rather different lines:

Informing executives and supervisors from time to time about the company profit picture, and the spread that is needed between costs and

[5] This section summarizes the major findings of Chapter 3, pp. 39-44.

4

sales to maintain profits. But this does not require incorporating profit information in the periodic accounting reports, or arbitrarily allocating overhead items to individual statements.

Developing further the problem-solving uses of accounting information which will help to educate executives and supervisors as to the profit consequences of specific decisions.

ORGANIZATION WITHIN THE CONTROLLER'S DEPARTMENT [6]

There is generally much to be gained from separating, to a considerable degree within the controller's department, the personnel and units responsible for each of three major kinds of functions:

Bookkeeping, and preparation and distribution of periodic accounting reports.

Assistance to the operating departments in current analyses of accounting information for score-card and attention-directing purposes.

Participation in the use of accounting information for problem solving on a special-studies basis.

Perhaps the principal need for separating these functions is to maintain adequate administrative direction and control over the amount of time and effort that is devoted to the different kinds of tasks by accounting personnel. It was repeatedly observed that, when accountants had heavy supervisory responsibilities for report preparation in addition to analytical responsibilities, the pressures of supervision and deadlines led to a relative neglect of analytical work. As a result, when the functions are combined, the controller's department retains little control over the amount of effort that is given to each.

Combining the functions leads to a potential conflict between the accountant's function of providing service to operating departments, and his function of analyzing operations to provide valid and objective data for higher levels of management. Separating the record-keeping functions from analytical work is also an important supplement to an effective internal audit in reducing the dangers of collusion. It may also give the analytical personnel greater freedom to develop close working relationships with operating executives without a feeling of conflicting responsibilities.

Another reason for separating the functions is to allow greater flexibility for organizing each of them in the most economical and effective manner. If there is some organizational separation, each function can be located at the level or levels most appropriate for its particular task. Each can be centralized or decentralized to the extent that appears desirable, independently of the others.

CENTRALIZATION AND DECENTRALIZATION: CURRENT ANALYSIS [7]

An essential condition for the attention-directing use of data is that the accounting reports be reviewed regularly and periodically in order to determine when

[6] This section summarizes the major findings of Chapter 4, pp. 60-71.
[7] This section summarizes the major findings of Chapter 4, pp. 45-56, and Chapter 5, pp. 72-76.

performance is "off standard" and to initiate inquiries as to the reasons. A principal means for accomplishing this lies in the development of communication channels between the controller's department and the operating departments at the appropriate levels.

There are at least two directions in which the controller's department can take the initiative to strengthen the use of accounting services:

By doing an effective job of funneling reports upward from factories and sales units, and bringing them to the attention of top level executives, so that these executives, in turn, will use the reports in dealing with their subordinates.

By getting top management support for a regular, systematic interpretation of monthly cost variances to be prepared by operating men with the assistance of analysts from the accounting department. This will encourage a regular and growing contact between the controller's department and operating men at middle management levels.

Among the most essential direct communications channels between controller's and operating departments are those between the controller and the factory department head, the factory manager, the district and regional sales managers, and the top company executives responsible for production and sales.

Such channels can be developed by:

Giving accounting personnel duties that can only be discharged by working with operating men.

Giving these assignments high priority by separating them from record-keeping and supervisory functions.

Physically locating the accounting man close to his operating counterpart.

Using for these contacts accounting personnel who have adequate status and character to maintain the relationships on a basis of mutual respect, and who possess a thorough understanding of operations.

CENTRALIZATION AND DECENTRALIZATION: SPECIAL STUDIES [8]

In the companies studied, a very great part of the "spade work" in investigating major operating problems is done by persons outside the controller's department; hence, to a large extent, these problems cut across departmental lines and have to be dealt with from a company-wide or factory-wide viewpoint. For this reason, the special studies work calls for more centralized communications than the current analysis work. An effective organizational arrangement appears to be to establish a unit for special studies in the company offices of the controller's department, and a smaller unit of the same sort in each of the larger factories or other major operating units.

Under most circumstances *the controller's department can most effectively bring its special skills to bear upon problems as a part of a team — formal or informal — that includes staff assistants to operating executives and members of other staff departments as well as accounting personnel.*

[8] This section summarizes the major findings of Chapter 4, pp. 56-60.

Formal procedures that required the preparation of "savings statements" as a basis for capital appropriations were very effective in bringing the controller's department into the decision-making process. Institution of a formal cost reduction program had this same general effect. This suggests that the use of accounting information for problem-solving purposes could be further extended by developing similar procedures in areas like production scheduling, market research, or quality control, which would give the controller's department a broader opportunity to participate formally in the investigatory process. It would also increase effective managerial use of the wealth of data available from the controller's department.

CENTRALIZATION AND DECENTRALIZATION: RECORD KEEPING[9]

For the record-keeping units, the main questions of centralization and decentralization relate to the geographical location of the personnel. How far should the record-keeping and reporting functions be centrally located? How far should they be decentralized to factories and sales districts?

The most important consequences of centralization or decentralization of the records functions have to do with the accessibility of documents and the reliability of the source records. Both of these criteria point in the direction of relatively great geographical decentralization. To give access to detailed records, it is generally advantageous to decentralize record keeping to the locations where the major uses are made of the data. To get reliability, the accounting personnel who are responsible for recording and classifying data need to be as close as possible to the operating situations where the data originate.

There may be definite cost advantages in centralizing to the extent that is necessary for mechanization or clerical specialization. In the surveyed operations, most of these economies can be attained with units centralized to the factory or regional sales level. Further centralization apparently offers little additional gain from a a cost standpoint. For this reason it should be possible to retain most of the advantages of decentralization mentioned in the previous paragraph without decentralizing so far as to incur serious clerical "diseconomies."

Questions of promptness, uniformity in classification of data, and auditing control are in most instances of small importance in determining the optimal degree of centralization and decentralization of record keeping.

Manufacturing Records

For manufacturing operations of any size, the volume of clerical work in a single factory is generally sufficient to permit the bulk of the accounting for manufacturing operations to be done at the factory. There remains the question of whether factory record-keeping activities should be further subdivided and decentralized into accounting units paralleling the several operating departments in the factory, or whether they should be assigned to centralized units corresponding to the major accounting activities. The conclusion reached from survey observations is that the net advantage lies on the side of the centralized structure within the factory, al-

[9] This section summarizes the major findings of Chapter 4, pp. 60-68, and Chapter 5, pp. 76-80 and pp. 89-94.

7

though the balance of advantages is less decisive in a very large factory with several separate products and production lines, than it is in a smaller factory.

When the purchasing function is centralized for the company as a whole, the question arises as to whether the accounts payable work should be handled in the company offices or the individual factories. The project staff were unable to determine that there were important advantages, one way or another.

Sales Records

In sales accounting, the operations involving the greatest volume of clerical work are billing and the maintenance of accounts receivable. There are indications that, primarily for reasons of access to records, evident advantages exist in locating the accounts receivable in the same city or cities as the credit units. But to achieve clerical economy in posting to the accounts, the credit work should not be further decentralized than is absolutely necessary.

In none of these companies was the location of billing a particularly critical matter. When sales are made through company sales branches, locating the billing function with accounts receivable and collections seems generally satisfactory. In other cases, the advantages seem fairly balanced between billing at the factory or sending a copy of the shipping memorandum to a central billing unit located with accounts receivable.

FORMAL AUTHORITY OVER DECENTRALIZED ACCOUNTING OPERATIONS [10]

There are two general types of arrangements of the lines of formal authority in the companies studied. In some, the factory controller or chief accounting executive [11] is completely under the formal authority of the company controller. In other companies he is "functionally" responsible to the company controller, "administratively" to the factory manager.

It was observed that when the accounting department lacks acceptance and active support from the top levels of the manufacturing department, it may be unsatisfactory to divide authority over the factory accountant between the company controller and the factory manager. But in organizations *where top executives of the operating departments regard the controller's services as important management tools, a system of divided authority appears to work as well as a plan in which the factory controller or district office manager reports solely to the company controller.*

Of greater importance than the lines of formal authority is the question of how much leeway should be given the accounting man, at a decentralized location, to run his own shop. Whether authority was centralized or decentralized, *it was found that the greatest service was provided to factory management when the factory accountant felt that he had authority to provide reports to the factory management as*

---

[10] This section summarizes the main findings of Chapter 5, pp. 80-89.

[11] To avoid confusion of terms and to reduce necessity for lengthy, qualifying phrases, the term "factory accountant" is used in this report to designate the chief accounting and control executive in the factory. This is not intended to suggest that a division or factory controller's responsibilities are confined to accounting.

requested, within the minimum standards of accounting policy and procedure laid down by the company controller's department.

Whatever the formal arrangements, it seemed that appointments and removals of factory accountants are almost always a matter of negotiation and agreement between the controller's department and the factory manager. Admitting this joint responsibility, there is probably some advantage in placing the formal power of appointment in the controller's department.

Because of the nature of their duties, office managers in sales groups are more likely than factory accountants to regard themselves, and to be regarded, as members of the operating executive's staff. On the whole, the case for decentralized authority appears stronger in the sales than in the manufacturing area. But, where the normal lines of personnel movement lie within the accounting department, the office managers themselves tend to prefer having personnel and salary administration in the hands of the controller's department.

THE DEVELOPMENT OF ACCOUNTING PERSONNEL [12]

In most organizations, promotion tends to be more or less "vertical." When a position is vacant, the tendency is to fill it by promotion from one of the positions immediately subordinate to it, or in a related part of the organization. If an organization is designed along the lines recommended above, a vertical promotion policy is likely to lead to difficulties. With the separation between analytical work and record-keeping functions, one group of accounting executives would, with vertical promotion, develop their analytical skills but acquire little experience in supervision; another group would acquire supervisory skills with little chance to develop competence in analytical work.

Hence, *in an organization developed along the suggested lines, it is important that there be an intelligent and carefully administered plan for the horizontal transfer of potential supervisors and executives at several stages of their careers.* By horizontal transfer is meant promotion from analytic positions to supervisory positions in record-keeping units, and vice versa.

Personnel development for controllership functions is an organizational problem only to a limited degree. To a far greater extent it is a problem of providing men with training and experience, both prior to and during their employment, that will deepen and broaden their understanding of general business problems. One specific direction for progress is the broadening of pre-employment training for industrial accountants. A second direction is to develop further the opportunities for interdepartmental promotion of promising men. A third direction is to encourage the use of teams and "task forces" drawn from several departments to undertake major planning studies.

THE CONTROLLER'S DEPARTMENT IN A MODERN BUSINESS CONCERN

Although this study has been concerned primarily with the internal organization of the controller's department, the survey team would like to record the observation that, from a long-range standpoint, some of the important questions of

[12] This section summarizes the main findings of Chapter 6, pp. 95-104.

9

organization can only be decided in terms of the rôle that the controller's department and the accounting profession are going to play in the over-all management picture. If that rôle is restricted largely to accounting and the preparation of figures to be analyzed by others, a relatively centralized organization may operate in a satisfactory manner. But if the controller's department undertakes larger responsibilities for analytical and advisory work, a correspondingly greater degree of decentralization is called for.

In the long run, the division of functions will probably depend on the capacity of the professions providing personnel for these departments. If so, the future organizational patterns will be much influenced by what the industrial accounting profession makes of itself. If it can attract men of superior competence and broad training, these are likely to lead to larger responsibilities for the profession.

Chapter 2

POSING THE PROBLEM OF ORGANIZATION

Summary

This chapter provides the necessary background for findings reported in the succeeding chapters of the report. It has been said that a problem correctly stated is half solved. The first section of the chapter, therefore, presents the setting of the problem by describing briefly the range of accounting and control functions with which the research is concerned. This section will help to make clear what is meant by accounting and controllership services to management.

The second and main section of the chapter presents a careful statement of the meaning of the terms "centralization" and "decentralization" as used in this study. In the course of clarifying the meaning of these terms, some of the important questions of organization emerge. Consideration is also given to the ways in which organization structure relates to centralization and decentralization of decisions. Finally, there is a brief description of the extent of centralization or decentralization of the seven surveyed companies.

CONTROLLERSHIP FUNCTIONS IN THE SURVEYED COMPANIES

Since we are interested primarily in the use of figures by management, we shall exclude certain important functions commonly handled by controller's departments — for example, tax accounting and financial reporting to stockholders.

Common Functions

With due allowance for some differences in emphasis, there was a remarkable similarity in the kinds of functions performed by the controller's departments of the seven companies studied. In general, they performed the functions commonly associated with controllership.[1] In addition to accounting functions, each of these departments also participated in the policy-making and decision-making processes in a variety of ways. To a greater or lesser extent, controller's department personnel assist personnel of other departments (such as sales and production) in analyzing and interpreting accounting, statistical, and operating data. All seven controller's departments participate in, or conduct, special analyses which are directly related to policy decisions. The controllers or their key assistants also are active as members of policy committees.

[1] See, for example, David R. Anderson, *Practical Controllership* (Chicago: Irwin, 1947), Chapter 1; and Controllers Institute of America, *Answering Your Questions About Controllers Institute*.

The core of functions common to all these controllers' departments — accounting, broadly defined — becomes the common denominator of this study, and its focusing point. Such treatment is simply an effective analytical tool. It is not intended to suggest that controllership is restricted to accounting, however broadly defined. The next paragraphs indicate briefly to what extent the scope of responsibility for these functions differed in the seven companies. It will become clear that the differences were relatively slight in relation to the large area of common functions.

Some Basic Differences in Functions Performed

Two areas in which considerable variation was found in allocating functions between the controller's department and other departments are:

Recording of time and production in factory accounting, and
Credit and collections.

Recording of time and production. Regardless of *who* records them, the original time and production records must be decentralized to the factory. In the factories of several companies, production data are initially recorded by foremen or clerks in the operating departments. This is generally true, for example, in the iron and steel making departments at Donora Works and National Works. In other factories, inspectors in the inspection department record production data. The Standard Control Division at Westinghouse provides an example of this practice. In at least five of the factories, and in some departments of others, the initial production records were made by clerks in the accounting department, usually located in the actual production centers. This is the practice, for example, in the two H. J. Heinz factories and the Etna Works of the National Supply Company.

The problems associated with the initial recording of production data will be discussed further in the chapter on factory accounting. The size of clerical staffs required in the factory accounting departments of these companies varies greatly because of the different ways in which this function is handled. For this reason, among others, a simple comparison of the costs of operating the controllers' departments is not a valid measure of relative efficiency.

Credit and collections. Responsibilities for credit and collections are shared in various ways among the controllers' departments, sales departments, and treasurers' departments. Three examples will illustrate the range of organization practice observed. At Eastman Kodak, a credit and accounts receivable bookkeeping section in the controller's department is completely responsible for checking credit ratings and authorizing credit; the same unit maintains the accounts receivable ledgers. In H. J. Heinz, each sales branch passes on credit, and the branch office manager ("administratively" responsible to the sales manager, "functionally" to the controller) maintains the accounts receivable records. At National Suppy, divisional credit managers, in the treasurer's department, make the credit investigations and decisions. They are independent of both the controller and the sales manager. The problems associated with the organization of credit and collections will be discussed further in the sections on sales accounting.

Other Differences in Functions

In several cases — two will be noted specifically — functions not usually considered controllership functions are under the formal authority of the controller. At H. J. Heinz, those *production scheduling* tasks performed at the factories are located in the factory accounting department. At the Kodak Park Works of Eastman Kodak, *industrial engineering* is located in the controller's division. In both cases, however, these activities are carried on in semi-independent subdepartments, and the relationships between the personnel responsible for these functions and the accounting personnel are similar to those in the other surveyed companies. In this study, therefore, they are considered "other staff departments."

Finally, it is common practice in surveyed companies to assign rather broad office management responsibilities to the accounting units in regional and district sales offices.[2] It is not practicable to draw a sharp line between the accounting and non-accounting responsibilities of these sales accounting units.

THE MEANING OF CENTRALIZATION AND DECENTRALIZATION

"Centralization" is a word of many meanings. With reference to management problems, an administrative organization is *centralized* to the extent that decisions are made at relatively high levels in the organization, and persons at lower levels have relatively little discretion. Conversely, an administrative organization is *decentralized* to the extent that important delegations of discretionary and decision-making authority are made from higher to lower levels of the organization.

This study is particularly concerned with:

The degree of centralization or decentralization within the controller's department;

The relationship of this to the degree of centralization or decentralization within operating departments, particularly manufacturing and sales.

Centralization and Decentralization in Controllers' Departments

In some companies a factory accountant is given broad discretion to determine the accounting procedures to be used in the factory, or the kinds of reports to be prepared for the factory manager; in other companies, he is not. In the former case, therefore, there is relatively great decentralization *to the factory level* within the controller's department; in the latter situation there is relatively great centralization *to the company level* within the controller's department.

Centralization and Decentralization in Operating Departments

In some companies a factory manager is given broad discretion to determine manufacturing methods, to handle industrial relations, even, in some cases, to determine what the factory is to produce. The broader the scope of the functions over which the factory manager exercised discretion, the greater the decentraliza-

---

[2] Certain office management functions are also performed by the works accounting department at Donora and National Works.

tion *to the factory level* in the manufacturing department. In several of the companies studied (Westinghouse Electric is an example) there is an important intermediate stage of delegation between the company level and the factory level — the division. Certain matters are decentralized all the way to the factory, others only to the division. Similarly, on the sales side, in many companies the regional office constitutes an important level between the central company office on the one hand, and the district sales office, on the other.

Relationship Between Controller and Operating Department Decentralization

Effectiveness of centralization or decentralization of the controller's department is likely to depend on the relative centralization of operating departments of the company, particularly manufacturing and sales. For example, there would be little apparent point in supplying department foremen with information that would help them schedule production if scheduling decisions are made at the factory or company level with little departmental participation.

What constitutes an effective relationship between the controller's department and operating departments? Is the most effective procedure to feed accounting, statistical and analytical information into the operating organization at the levels where the relevant operating decisions are being made? Or is it better to feed all accounting information in at the top levels of the operating organization, relying on the manufacturing and sales executives to transmit downward information needed for decisions at lower levels. How far should the analysis of data be an accounting responsibility; how far an operating responsibility? It is clear, then, that the study involves examination of centralization and decentralization of the broad accounting functions of controllership *in relation to* operating centralization and decentralization.

Degree and Elements of Centralization or Decentralization Are the Core of the Problem

Centralization may also vary within an administrative unit, some of its functions being centralized while others are decentralized. None of the seven companies studied had completely centralized organizations and functions. Particular activities within the seven companies were found to be centralized or decentralized *to a degree,* varying widely from unit to unit, and from function to function. Thus, posing the problem of centralization became a question of examining the *degree* of centralization and decentralization of the different decision-making functions. It also involved analyzing the *impact* of centralization on five important elements of accounting functions of the controller's department:

1. The *structure of the accounts and reports.* For example, whether the chart of accounts is broken down in such a way that a cost statement or a profit and loss statement can be drawn up for an individual factory or department within a factory.

2. The actual *geographical locations* where accounting functions are performed. For example, whether the records of factory costs are posted at the factory or in the company offices.

3. The *formal authority relations* between accounting personnel and operating personnel. For instance, whether the factory accountant reports to the company controller or to the factory manager.

4. The structure of *group loyalties.* Whether the factory accounting personnel regard themselves as part of the factory "team" or as part of the controller's department, for example.

5. The *channels used* by accounting and operating personnel *in communicating* with each other. For instance, whether the company controller and his home office subordinates communicate directly with the factory controller, or whether their communications with the factory are channeled through the factory manager.

The following paragraphs will attempt to clarify further what is meant by each of these five elements.

Decentralization of accounts and reports. The first element relates to the structure of the accounts and reports themselves. For example, in a company with a number of factories, the account structure is decentralized to the factory level if most costs for a factory are separately accumulated and a more or less complete income and expense statement prepared periodically for the factory. Similarly, if within each factory costs are accumulated for each department, the structure is decentralized down to the departmental level.

Decentralization of the accounting structure is aimed at the greatest possible decentralization of operating decisions but retaining the operating executive's responsibility for results — results that may be measured in terms of sales, profits, return on investment, or cost reduction.[3]

The idea that the account structure should be decentralized at least to the factory has gained wide acceptance in American industry. In selecting companies for study, the project staff was unable to discover one that did not go at least this far in decentralizing its accounts. Almost all accounting and operating executives of these companies were agreed that the factory manager's job is to make as large a profit as possible, within the limits of company policy, with the manufacturing facilities and investment available to him.

The device most generally used in these companies for securing accountability with a decentralized account structure is the budget, usually of the flexible type, and a monthly comparison of actual with budgeted expenditures. In most, but not all the companies, the determinants of the monthly production cost allowances are tied in directly to the system of standard production costs, adjusted for volume variance. Thus, when the actual manufacturing cost equals the standard, the actual expenditure equals the budget. In about half the companies, a profit and loss statement is prepared for each factory or group of factories in a division. Practice varies as to whether sales are entered in the factory profit and loss statement at actual sales price or at a standard price. One company calculates for each factory the ratio of profits to investment; another is planning to introduce a balance sheet prorating its total capital investment to its various manufacturing facilities, and treating each, on paper, as a separate "corporation."

Generally, decentralization of accounts is not carried as far in sales as in manufacturing. In one case, the manufacturing department "sells" its product to the

[3] For a nontechnical discussion of the philosophy underlying decentralization of the account structure, see Perrin Stryker, "P & C for Profit," *Fortune,* April 1952, pp. 128 ff.

sales department, and profit and loss statements are prepared for geographically decentralized sales units, but this is not general practice.

There is a wide range in the degree of completeness of the factory accounts. At one end of the range is a company in which purchasing of principal raw materials is centralized. The factory accounts show only the labor actually employed at the factory and operating supplies purchased locally. Material costs and allocations of the company sales and administrative expenses do not appear on the factory statements.

At the other end of the range is a company in which the factory statements include all manufacturing expenses, including materials priced at standard, together with a recirculated allocation of company sales and administrative expenses. The companies which have carried furthest the philosophy of fixing profit responsibility at the factory tend toward this structure of factory accounts.

Geographical centralization and decentralization. A second, and quite distinct element in decentralization is the *geographical dispersion* of bookkeeping and accounting functions to the actual locations where manufacturing and sales activities are carried on. It was this characteristic that a controller had in mind when he stated in an interview: "We have decentralized our factory cost figures. They keep their own records."

There is, of course, no necessary connection between the degree of decentralization of the account structure, as previously defined, and the geographical decentralization of accounting activities. It would be entirely possible to have the account structure decentralized to the departments, for example, and still have all of the original accounting documents forwarded to the central company offices for recording and preparation of reports. On the other hand, it would also be entirely possible to have virtually all the recording activities, including tabulating, carried on at the plants and district sales offices, but no separate cost reports prepared for these individual organizational units.

As a matter of fact, in the companies studied, those that have gone furthest in decentralization of their accounts and reports have generally gone furthest in geographical decentralization of accounting functions. This raises the question, to be discussed in later chapters, of whether there are compelling administrative reasons why these two aspects of decentralization should go hand in hand. Will the efficiency or effectiveness of accounting suffer if there is more or less geographical decentralization than decentralization of accounts? Or has this close connection come about simply through a lack of recognition that two separate sets of organizational decisions are involved here?

In the companies studied, a number of situations existed where these two kinds of decentralization have not been carried to the same organizational levels. The case of accounts receivable in Eastman Kodak has already been mentioned. Although the *accounts* are decentralized so that reports can be compiled for individual sales branches, the accounts receivable ledgers are maintained and posted in the company central offices. Comparison of National Works with Donora Works yields an example of varying practice in factory departments. The account structure is very similar in the two works, but at Donora many of the recording functions are handled by accounting units located out in the several works de-

16

partments, while at National most of these functions are performed at the central works accounting offices.

Centralization and decentralization of authority. A third element in centralization and decentralization relates to the lines of formal authority in the organization. Viewing a multi-plant (or multi-division) company as a whole, it is decentralized if each factory operates as a more or less self-contained unit, with the factory manager responsible for all of the functions carried on within the factory, and having formal authority over all factory personnel.

If the industrial relations director in the factory or the head of the industrial engineering department reports to his counterpart in the company offices, instead of to the factory manager, the organization is centralized to that extent. Similarly, if the top accounting executive in the factory reports formally to the factory manager, accounting control is decentralized; if he reports to the company controller, it is centralized.

Again, this third element in centralization and decentralization may be quite independent of the two previously examined. Indeed, in the companies studied, decentralization of the account structure and geographical decentralization of accounting functions had always been carried further than the decentralization of authority.

In answering questions about formal authority, persons interviewed usually made a distinction between "administrative" authority and "functional" authority. By "administrative" authority they meant the day-to-day relation of a "boss" to his subordinates. This included work assignments, handling personnel and operating questions referred by subordinates, and settling questions involving relations among subordinates. By "functional" authority they meant the right to determine the technical aspects of the accounting function: the chart of accounts, report content and deadlines, bookkeeping procedures, and so on. Obviously, there is some possibility of overlap and of disagreement as to precisely which decisions fall in one category and which in the other. However, little confusion or disagreement was found in the operating departments as to the proper classification of matters which arose in daily operation.

In three companies — General Mills (Food Division), and the American Steel and Wire and National Tube Divisions of U. S. Steel — the factory accounting executive is both administratively and functionally responsible to the company controller. As one company controller put it: "The responsibility of the company controller extends into the factory. It is a solid line." The company controller's authority in these cases includes the right to hire and fire the factory accounting executive. These three companies are the most centralized from the standpoint of formal authority.

In H. J. Heinz, National Supply and Eastman Kodak, the factory accounting executive is administratively responsible to the factory manager, functionally responsible to the company controller. In Westinghouse, the division controller recognizes a "solid-line" responsibility to the company controller, a "dotted-line" responsibility to the division manager. In reality, however, the distinction between Westinghouse and the other three "decentralized" companies is not substantial.

In the five companies where the study covered sales accounting (it did not in the National Tube and American Steel and Wire Divisions) formal authority over

17

sales accounting managers in regional and district offices is divided in the same general way as authority over factory accountants. However, it should be noted that there is less geographical decentralization of sales accounting than of factory accounting. Hence, the head of the company sales accounting division tends to have broader administrative authority over personnel performing these functions than does his counterpart for factory accounting.

Group loyalties. The formal authority relationships do not tell the whole story of whether the factory accountant operates as a member of a centralized accounting department or a member of a decentralized factory staff. His personal feelings of loyalty must be taken into account. On the organization chart, he might appear as a member of the accounting department, but in fact he might regard himself as a part of the factory management team; the reverse might be true.

It is not easy, in an interview with strangers, for a member of an organization to give a frank and objective appraisal of where his loyalties lie. Hence, the survey team attempted to assess a number of related pieces of evidence to learn whether factory accountants regarded themselves primarily as members of the factory manager's "team" or the company controller's "team." For example, they were asked which of two reporting assignments with close deadlines would receive priority. The interviewer noted whether they spoke of the operating management of the factory as "we" or "they," and similarly, for the home-office accounting department. Whether or not informal lunch-time and other social groups tended to cut across the line between accounting and operations was observed and noted.

Appraisal of this evidence indicates that loyalty tends to be closely associated with the centralization or decentralization of formal authority. In general, the primary loyalty of the factory accountant is with the controller's department in those companies where formal authority in accounting is centralized. In those companies where formal authority is decentralized, the loyalties appear, on balance, to be with factory management. There were two factories, among those in companies with decentralized authority, where the factory accountants felt themselves more or less cut off from *both* the factory management and the controller's department. In these two situations, the factory accountants tended to regard themselves as subject to "cross pressure" from these two sources, rather than as having a strong allegiance to either.

The sample of seven companies and nine factories is far too small to permit a generalized assessment of the factors associated with centralized or decentralized loyalties and their relative importance. A few observations may be mentioned as explanatory factors.

Geographical separation from the home office appears to foster decentralized loyalties. In companies having distant branches, in California, for example, comments were frequently volunteered about the problems of maintaining home-office control over accounting operations in those branches.

Further, the feeling that "we are accountants, but they are operating people," appears to be a powerful force restraining the decentralization of accounting loyalties. Even in the situations with most decentralized loyalties, the accounting personnel felt strongly their responsibility for accurate reporting in accordance with *company* accounting procedures — including procedures they thought incorrect or inadequate.

18

A number of specific instances were observed where competing claims were made upon accounting personnel to adhere to the professional standards of accountancy on the one hand and, on the other, to get along with factory management by not reporting unpleasant facts. With one possible exception, all observed conflicts of this sort were resolved in favor of the standards of the profession.

Centralized loyalties were also fostered by the tendency of accounting personnel to look to the controller's department for chances of promotion. Except for Eastman Kodak, there was little transfer of accounting employees into manufacturing departments; there was more movement into sales department positions. Where interdepartmental promotions were relatively common, loyalties were more decentralized than elsewhere. Whether the opportunities for promotion are the cause, and the decentralized loyalties the effect, or *vice versa,* is hard to assess.

Centralization and decentralization of communication. Closely related to the question of centralization or decentralization of formal authority and of feelings of loyalty is the question of communications. Communications aspects of accounting organization will be considered decentralized to the factory if communications of the factory accounting personnel are more frequent with factory operating executives than with the headquarters controller's department. In the opposite case, the organization is considered centralized. Further, communication is not considered to be the routine flow of accounting documents and reports, but contacts by letter, telephone, or face-to-face for the purpose of assigning work, requesting information, settling problems of accounting procedure, and so forth. Both the amount and importance of such communication will be taken into account in assessing relative strength of communication channels.

As with other elements in decentralization, the pattern of communications within a plant or division may differ significantly from the organization of accounting communication for the company as a whole. At least one situation was found where communication for the *company as a whole* was relatively centralized — that is, communications between headquarters and factory control and accounting. However, *within the factory,* communication was relatively decentralized — in the sense that there was more communication between the factory accounting department and other factory departments than between the accounting department and the factory manager.

Referring to communications between company controller and factory accounting executives, the differences in degree of centralization among the surveyed companies is not spectacularly large, but it is noticeable. General Mills (Food Division) is probably the most centralized. Next in order of centralization are American Steel and Wire, National Supply, and National Tube — which form an intermediate group with a fairly narrow spread. At the decentralized end of the spectrum are Westinghouse, H. J. Heinz, and Eastman Kodak, the latter providing the example of greatest decentralization.

SIGNIFICANCE FOR CENTRALIZATION OR DECENTRALIZATION OF OPERATIONS

Having described these five elements of the relationship between accounting and operating centralization and decentralization, what is their significance for operations, considered separately? Take the case of a factory manager in a multi-plant company. Decentralization of accounts is aimed at presenting a separate, and relatively self-contained accounting picture of the operations of an individual factory or other major operating unit. The other four elements — location of accounting functions, formal authority, group loyalties, and communications — are aimed at making the factory accounting department an integral part of the factory organization, and giving the factory manager broad responsibility for a relatively complete and self-contained administrative organization.

Theoretically, the five elements are independent. Some of the controllers interviewed pointed out that decentralization in one element by no means implied that decentralization in other aspects was either necessary or desirable. On the relation between the account structure and geographical decentralization, one said:

"We have decentralized the accounts to the factory. We make a profit and loss statement for each factory; but the statement is actually prepared in the company offices, for we have the problem of allocating selling and administrative expenses. That distribution is made here."

This same controller thought that if the factory accountant were given broader discretion to adapt the factory accounting procedures and reports to the needs of the factory manager, this step would need to be balanced by a greater centralization of formal authority over the factory accountant in order to protect consistency of the accounting system as a whole:

"If we moved completely over to decentralization (in geographical location of activities), I think I might want the factory accountant to report directly to me."

Actually, there is a relatively close relationship among the five elements of decentralization in the surveyed companies. Decentralization in one aspect frequently accompanies decentralization in the others. For example, with respect to each one of the five elements, General Mills (Food Division) is more centralized than Eastman Kodak. In particular, the three companies described as having relatively centralized formal authority are also relatively centralized with respect to communications. Three of the four companies with decentralized formal authority have relatively decentralized communications. Relations of formal authority were closely associated, in turn, with group loyalties. Finally, when accounting personnel are geographically decentralized, decentralization of communications and group loyalty are thereby encouraged.

Observations indicate that the relationships probably mutually reinforce each other. If the lines of formal authority run in a centralized direction — that is, to the company accounting department — this tends to strengthen loyalties running in the same direction and to encourage communication in that direction. Or if there is a great deal of communication between factory accounting personnel and operating personnel, this tends to develop group loyalties and the group loyalties to encourage further communication. In this way, decentralization of communication contributes to decentralization of loyalties, and *vice versa*.

It was impossible to determine precisely which are the causal factors in the situation. The fact that there is a high correlation among the five elements makes this question less important than it would be if each element in decentralization were completely independent of the others.

In fact one of the major difficulties encountered in the study was to discover

20

companies that would represent a sufficiently wide range of centralized and decentralized situations. In manufacturing concerns of any size with multiple factory locations, the accepted philosophy seems to be that expenditures incurred at the factory should generally be accounted for at the factory, and that revenues and other costs should be allocated to the individual factories. Since these two conditions held in all of the companies studied, the principal variables studied were those relating to the last three of the five elements in centralization — that is: centralization and decentralization of formal authority, group loyalties, and communications. The central question is how these affect the operating effectiveness of the accounting system.

Chapter 3

THE USE OF FIGURES BY MANAGEMENT

Summary

This chapter reports principal findings about use (or non-use) of accounting data by operating executives and supervisors. These findings show how important it is for the controller to have a clear picture of the way in which operating decisions are made, and where in the organizational structure such decisions are made. They suggest, further, that by making a distinction between score-card, attention-directing and problem-solving uses of data, the controller can gain valuable insight into the most suitable and effective ways for presenting reports and analyses for use by operating executives and their departments. The findings also suggest that the controller of any company could improve these services. This could be done by survey interviews with an adequate sample of operating men. Such interviews should be conducted along lines similar to those of this study; they should be designed to get at the accounting data and reports wanted by operating men as tools to help them manage and control *their* particular operation.

How accounting data are used. Interviews with accounting and operating personnel indicate that accounting data may be used:

As a sort of *score card* for the over-all appraisal of an operating unit.

To *direct attention* to problems that need to be solved.

To aid in the actual *solution of problems.*

It should be noted that specific accounting data may have different facets of interest and use for various executives. Some examples will help to illustrate these points.

In one company, an annual calculation is made for each factory of the ratio of profit earned by that factory to investment in factory facilities. For the plant manager this has a *score-card* value. If he earns a high percentage of profit, or if his profit goes up from one year to the next, he is likely to feel that he is doing a good job. If the profit is low or goes down, he is likely to be encouraged to additional effort. In some cases, the use of the accounting results as the basis for a supervisory bonus emphasizes the score-card function. Note that in these cases, the accounting figures act as a stimulus, but do not help the manager decide what can or should be done.

This very same figure, the factory's rate of return on investment, is used by top management in this company as an *attention director*. Those factories which consistently turn up with low or declining profit percentages are regarded as trouble spots requiring special attention from the company executives. In those factories where the rate of return is regarded as satisfactory, the manager is left rather free to run his own show. For the company management, therefore, the return figure is more than a score-card record. It also directs attention to operating units which need special analysis and review. Thus, the same item of information may be an attention director for one executive but primarily a score card for others, or it may have both score-card and attention-directing utility for the same person.

For example, take a factory general foreman or department head. His job consists in considerable part in "pushing" the work. He generally spends a large part of his time on the factory floor where he can actually observe the work being performed. He is concerned with seeing that jobs are filled, but that superfluous men are not on the payroll; that emergencies are met quickly and effectively, and delays minimized; that short-run, day-to-day problems of all sorts are handled promptly. His direct face-to-face contact with his subordinates and their work gives him many sources of information about what is going on, and he regards accounting information as only a supplement — and, in many instances, a not too important one — to the other sources. Accounting data are useful to him mainly in giving him a score card, summarizing for longer periods his day-to-day impressions. They also are useful in directing his attention to matters that are not visible and tangible — say, the rate of consumption of expendable tools, or of operating supplies.

In most of the companies, any appropriation for major new equipment has to be justified by an economy study or savings statement. This is an example of the "problem-solving" uses of accounting data. These uses go beyond the case where out-of-line accounting figures call attention to a problem or show in what area the problem lies. In problem-solving uses, the actual accounting data are inserted in the equation, so to speak, in order to solve the problem. Apart from plant and equipment studies, the most common examples of the problem-solving use of accounting data are in the comparison of profitability of product lines as a basis for a selective selling program, and the use of accounting data to forecast working capital requirements.

At higher levels of management the problem-solving uses of accounting data appear more commonly. For the vice president for manufacturing there are policy problems — developing and putting into production new products, plant location decisions, installation of new equipment and replacement of old, make-or-buy decisions, and so on. In many of these areas of decision, accounting data are used for problem-solving purposes. Sometimes they apparently are not used where they *could* be. They are used in preparation of special analyses or studies usually prepared by the executive's own assistants or by "staff" departments.[1] An equipment study, for example, would be most often made by the industrial engineering department. Sometimes, special studies are assigned to the controller's department and, even more frequently, that department is called on by other special-study units to supply the accounting data or dollar statistics needed for an analysis. Hence, the extent to which accounting data are used for problem-solving purposes depends very much on the kinds of staff assistance available to the vice president and on how much he is accustomed to use them.

Another concern of the manufacturing vice president is the evaluation and de-

[1] As is well known, "staff" is a slippery word that is perhaps best avoided altogether. In this publication the term is used simply as a shorthand way of referring to all the departments of a company other than manufacturing, sales, and engineering; and to all the departments of a factory other than the manufacturing and maintenance departments.

velopment of men. He needs to learn how his subordinates are doing, their strengths and their weaknesses. Moreover, the vice president has far less opportunity than the factory department head to observe his subordinates on the job. Hence, he is more dependent on reports as a basis for evaluating their progress and problems. He often uses accounting data and reports of internal auditors as a score card for his subordinates, and as a means of directing his attention to the areas where he needs to apply pressure or raise questions.

Observations made on this survey indicate that the score-card and attention-directing uses are apt to be more frequent than the problem-solving uses at all levels of management. First-line supervisors tend to use such data primarily as a fill-in on aspects of the work that they cannot appraise from actual contact. At higher levels, the data are used as a means of judging subordinates and as an independent check on what is happening at the operating level. Problem-solving uses of accounting data occur primarily in administrative units (staff units) for making analyses or special studies, for use by general management.

SCORE-CARD AND ATTENTION-DIRECTING USES OF DATA

It has been pointed out that no sharp line can be drawn between the score-card and the attention-directing uses of accounting data. What is a score card for the factory manager may be an attention director for the vice president for manufacturing; what is a score card for the regional sales manager may be an attention director for the general sales manager.

Illustrations of Score-Card and Attention-Directing Uses of Data

Here are some typical interview replies that illustrate the relation of the two uses. A general sales manager was asked:

"How do you tell when your regional managers are doing a good job?"

"The main things are the sales figures. Then, we've got to watch their expenses. Let's look at our weekly summary statistics. I see that the sales of X product are low compared to the quota. I go back to the regional report and see that New England is the low region, also which of the sales branches in the region are low. Then I know to whom to write a letter to follow it up."

One of the regional sales managers in the same company was asked: "How do you tell when you are doing a good job?" He replied: "I have a sales quota and an expense budget. I try to operate my region so that I will meet the quota or surpass it; and at the same time, I try to do the job in the most economical manner."

Necessary Distinctions: Data on Output, Expenditures and Efficiency

The interviews with operating executives show that the data used for score-card and attention-directing purposes depend partly on the nature of the data. For these purposes, it is convenient to classify the data into three groups:

Data on output. In manufacturing, the primary measures of output are production figures — expressed either in dollars or physical units. On the merchandising side, the primary measure is sales — again, either in physical or dollar terms. Most

24

other departments of a business do not have very satisfactory output measures. An engineering department might record the number of projects completed, but this is obviously an unsatisfactory unit of measure. In some cases (*e.g.,* number of purchase orders placed) certain aspects of output can be measured quantitatively, but in the nonmanufacturing, nonmerchandising units of a company, determination of results becomes largely a matter of qualitative judgment.

Data on expenditures. The bulk of the dollar figures recorded in the controller's department (apart from sales) falls in this category. Within limitations, expenditures can be allocated to various departments and units within departments of the company.

Data on efficiency. Efficiency means obtaining a given output with the least possible expenditure. An accounting system can produce data on efficiency only if two requirements are met:

Both output and expenditures can be measured.

A realistic, achievable standard of efficiency can be set.

The philosophy of cost accounting — orginally developed in relation to manufacturing operations — tends to focus on the use of accounting data for the control of efficiency. Our study shows that operating executives are quite as concerned with the control of output and the control of expenditures as with the control of their ratio. Note that in the example previously cited, neither the general sales manager nor the regional sales manager said he watched the *ratio* of sales to sales expenditures. Each said that he watched both the numerator (sales) and the denominator (sales expenses). Thus, whether operating supervisors and executives use accounting data for efficiency control depends on developing and presenting acceptable, usable data on efficiency.

To carry the story a step further, compare the control of efficiency in a factory having a well-developed cost accounting system with the control of output and expenses in a sales department. The comparison summarizes the way in which operating executives view accounting data in these two kinds of situations.

To the extent that factory executives have confidence in the accounting data as a valid measure of manufacturing efficiency, it is the analysis of the variance of actual costs from standard costs [2] which is of first importance. The factory manager does not decide what his volume of production shall be; this is determined for him.[3] His job, and the job of his department heads, is to achieve that production at the lowest possible cost. He is not limited by a fixed expenditure budget, but is expected to keep his expenditures in line with his output. The periodic cost statements are designed to measure how well this has been done.

The regional sales manager is not judged on the ratio between his sales and his sales expenditures; nor does he have the same range of discretion with respect to his budget as the factory manager. Instead, he is usually expected to operate *within* a fixed sales budget, and produce as large a volume of sales as possible.

---

[2] Here the term "standard cost" is used to mean the budgeted departmental (or factory) expenditure at actual volume and standard unit cost, rather than standard product costs, as in ordinary accounting usage.

[3] This is, of course, not literally true, and is approximately true only if the factory is operating well below capacity. See additional comments on pp. 37-39, about the distinction, from an accounting standpoint, between near-capacity and below-capacity operations.

Generally, for score-card and attention-directing purposes, operating executives interviewed seem to be as interested in watching data on output and on expenditures as they are in having the accounting department provide them with data on efficiency. This is even true to a considerable extent of manufacturing executives, and is true almost without exception in other areas of management.

With respect to manufacturing activities, an important reason is that the operating executives do not always accept, as valid measures of efficiency, the actual and standard costs that are reported to them. They would in many instances prefer to draw their own conclusions from the raw data as to whether expenditures are "high" or "low" in relation to output.

In nonmanufacturing activities, executives, almost without exception, are as interested (possibly more interested) in getting data on expenditures and on output as they are in having accounting provide them with data on efficiency. Measures of output that are adequate and that can be reasonably related to expenditures have not been invented.

Attention Directing and the "Principle of Exceptions"

The use of accounting data to call attention to problems is closely related to what is usually called "the principle of exceptions." For this procedure to work, the operating man must accept the validity of the standards for determining what is "out of line." Moreover, effective attention-directing uses of accounting data imply that it is through such data that problems are called to the attention of operating executives or general management.

Persons interviewed consistently reported that, in many instances where the production and sales executives *might* have had their attention directed to problems by accounting data, they had already learned of the problems from other sources before the accounting reports appeared. For example, delays due to equipment breakdown or material shortages are almost immediately brought to the attention of the foreman and usually the department head. If the problem is a serious one, the news travels upward rapidly, even to vice presidential and presidential levels. On these matters, accounting reports usually provide the supervisors with history but not with news.

On the other hand, in the course of his daily work even a first-line supervisor may find it difficult to learn that a particular machine logs excessive down-time because of mechanical failure. Here, a monthly summary of machine down-time with notation as to causes can be a valuable attention-directing report.

Interview data show conclusively that supervisors up to factory department heads use accounting reports for attention-directing purposes largely in areas that are not easily visible in the course of day-to-day supervision. The following comment of a factory department head is typical:

"Every day when I go out through the departments, I know the standard number of men who should be working on each operation. If I see more than the standard number working on a job, I check up to see why the extra people are there." "Couldn't you get that from the daily variance report?" "Yes, but I'd have to wait two days."

Operating supervisors were seldom able to cite other types of examples of the attention-directing services of the accounting system. On other items — direct labor, material usage, yield — the common reaction was: "We know all about that before the accounting reports come."

The following conclusions validly generalize survey information about attention-directing uses of accounting data by supervisors and executives who have direct contact with the factory floor or the sales market.

A large part of an operating executive's knowledge about his operation comes by direct observation and informal reports. These reports are frequently verbal and come to him through the regular supervisory channels. Accounting reports are only one, and not always the most important, of his sources of information, although they may be of considerable use in confirming his observations.

The operating executive has special needs for periodic accounting reports on items that are not "visible" from direct, day-to-day supervision. In manufacturing, machine performance and consumption of operating supplies are examples of such items.

For executives further removed from actual operations, the greatest significance of attention-directing accounting data lies in the information they transmit independently of operating supervisors. The existence of this independent source and channel of information has important consequences for the relations between executives at lower and higher levels.

Use of Data by Higher-Level Management

For other categories of executives — factory managers, regional sales managers, vice presidents, for example — the attention-directing uses of accounting data are somewhat different. Many of these executives feel a need for having some basis for keeping their subordinates alert, and for convincing them that "the boss knows what is going on." Since opportunities are limited for picking up information by actually observing the work, most of them pay considerable attention to accounting reports. A typical plant manager's comment on the monthly cost report is:

"This report will give me the deviations from standard for material yield, for direct labor, and for indirect labor. If something is making us not come out, I check and get the 'why.' The department head already knows he is going to have a variance, and usually he has a good reason."

In most factories, there is relatively little feeling that the factory manager is using the accounting statements as a mechanical or automatic score card for his subordinates. That is, most of the department heads believe that the variances are only one of a number of bases — usually not the most important — on which their superiors judge them; and the factory manager agrees with this.

The attitudes toward variances encountered almost uniformly among department heads included the following elements:

a. There is considerable pressure to avoid "red" variances because, even when they do not result from inefficient management by the department head, they have to be explained to his superior.

b. It is highly important to be able to provide an acceptable explanation of a "red" variance. "Explaining" may include: (1) indicating that corrective action was taken even before the situation came to the attention of the superior; and/or

27

(2) giving reasons for the variance which will not reflect upon departmental efficiency.

It is evident that attention-directing aspects of accounting reports are of considerable importance in the relationships between higher-level executives and their subordinates. Top executives can and do use the reports to show their subordinates that they know what is going on. Their subordinates give explanations of the variances in order to show their superiors that they also know what is going on. A typical comment by a department head:

"I look through them to get details on big variances. Those are for maintenance and material. I have to get the details if for no other reason than the monthly cost meeting, where I am called on to explain them."

Promptness of reports. The reaction of operating personnel to questions about the promptness of accounting reports permit some interesting generalizations. In the case of an accounting report which was not being used much and that was regarded as unimportant by the operators, interviewers generally got one of these two reactions: either the operator expressed himself as being entirely satisfied with the promptness of the report, or he used its lack of promptness as a rationalization for not using it.

The lesson to be learned from these interviews is that a very definite and specific picture must be obtained of the ways in which these reports can be and are used before considering the question of promptness or timeliness of accounting data and reports.

It has been noted that reports are used for their value in directing attention to trends and drifts, to underlying causes of recurrent day-to-day problems, and generally to matters that may escape attention in the course of direct supervision. To be effective as an attention director, a report must be in the hands of the operating man while happenings reflected in the report are still fresh in his mind. This enables him to give accurate, valid explanations when necessary. By and large, the significance of the reports lies in their *reminding* the operating executives of things they already know, and placing these things in proper quantitative perspective, rather than hinting to them things they never suspected and are unable to trace down to their causes.

A general rule of thumb that emerges from the interviews is that operating men think a report is sufficiently prompt if it is in their hands by the middle of the following reporting period. That is, if operating men want certain data on a daily basis, they generally feel that they ought to have it by the middle of the following day; weekly data, fairly early in the following week; monthly data, by the tenth or fifteenth day of the following month. Interviewers found substantially more use of daily reports in factories where reports were received within twelve hours than in factories where the reports were commonly two days late.

THE RÔLE OF STANDARDS [4]

When accounting data are used for score-card or for attention-directing purposes, a comparison of the actual data with some kind of standard or norm is al-

[4] Findings with respect to standards are in close agreement with other previous studies. See especially: John D. Glover and Fritz J. Roethlisberger, "Human Reactions to Standards and Controls," Ch. 8 in *Controllership in Modern Management*, T. F. Bradshaw and C. C. Hull (eds.), Chicago: Irwin, 1949; and Chris Argyris, *The Impact of Budgets on People*, New York: Controllership Foundation, Inc., 1952.

ways involved. This need not be a deliberately designed and established standard of the sort involved in a standard cost system, but may be any figure that is regarded as a "normal," "expected," "reasonable," or "satisfactory" value for the figure in question.

If an operating department head has become accustomed to "red" variances of $50,000 a month measured against the standard cost of his operation, then he is likely to regard a month in which his "red" variance is only $25,000 as a good one, even though the performance is still below standard. Similarly, a considerable number of executives were encountered whose real concern was not how they were making out with reference to the accounting standard, but how well they were doing in relation to historical records of past performance, or comparison with other plants in the same company.

Acceptance of Standards

Interview results show that a particular figure does not operate as a norm, in either a score-card or attention-directing sense, simply because the controller's department calls it a standard. It operates as a norm only to the extent that the executives and supervisors, whose activity it measures, accept it as a fair and attainable yardstick of their performance. Generally, operating executives were inclined to accept a standard to the extent that they were satisfied that the data were *accurately recorded*, that the standard level was *reasonably attainable*, and that the variables it measured were *controllable* by them. When there were doubts as to the accuracy of recording or classification of data, when the factors causing variances were thought to be beyond their own control, the executives simply did not believe that the standard validly measured their performance. Then they were influenced by it only to the extent that they were forced to think about the reactions of their superiors.

The degree of acceptance of standards was not the same, of course, in all the factories visited, nor even among different departments in the same factory. Some of the reasons for this are technical, and these will be discussed in the following paragraphs. In addition to the technical reasons, the length of time a cost system has been in operation has an important bearing on the validity and acceptability of standards. In all the companies studied, several years were required after the installation of a cost system before it was "shaken down" and a reasonably acceptable system of cost determinants arrived at. The same thing was observed in a case where a new processing department had recently been introduced in a factory which had a long-established cost system in its other departments.

It is not necessary to report on the degree to which standards were accepted in these various factories. As already mentioned, the range in level of acceptance was great. It is important, however, to learn what conditions have to be met so that accounting standards have a constructive influence upon operations, and how these conditions can be brought about through proper organizational relationships between the controller's department and the operating departments. For these reasons, the objections to existing accounting standards will be examined in some detail.

Two kinds of objections to standards were most frequently encountered. Some were criticisms of oversimplified determinants that failed to account for important external factors causing variability in costs. Thus, in several cases a cost that was only incurred during one season of the year received the same budget allowance per unit of output throughout the year. The fact that monthly variances in these cases were virtually meaningless tended to discredit the accounting standards and reports based on them.

In many instances the nature of the manufacturing operation practically precludes the establishment of adequate budget determinants. One problem frequently encountered is variation in the quality of raw materials. Food processing companies have continual difficulties of this kind, but similar troubles are found in other concerns. In companies like Westinghouse, where a standard cost often has to be estimated on each order, the task of arriving at acceptable and accepted standards is equally difficult.[5]

The recirculation of indirect costs was the second major source of distrust of accounting standards — and this on two scores. Almost all operating men stated their dislike at having on their statements items they did not regard as within their control. The objections were particularly strong when the items were not shown at standard, but caused variances on the statements.

Moreover, in the case of indirect items that were admitted to be partially controllable — maintenance expenditures, for example — doubts were frequently expressed as to the accuracy of the charges. In almost all companies there was a widespread belief (not entirely without foundation) that maintenance foremen inflated their time estimates to absorb idle time. As a matter of fact, at least one maintenance department head stated that he did just that: "Suppose the charges don't balance — there's $1,000 unallocated. Well, we know in X department they have some rough edges, so we shove that charge off on them." When clerical errors occur in charging supplies and maintenance to the proper accounts, they also feed this distrust.

In addition, there were frequent objections to the "lumpiness" of indirect charges. "You go along for months with favorable variances and then one month you'll take a licking." This sometimes led to the uneconomical ordering of small quantities of supplies, and pressure was often felt (and, fortunately, frequently resisted) to postpone necessary maintenance: "The machine was still not fixed and we were running out of our budget expense, but I didn't stop. They came around afterwards and said, 'You're way over your budget.' I said, 'Look out there. The machine is running, isn't it? Isn't that what the boss wants?' "

But a department head in another factory said, "I will sometimes pull back on some repairs when I think I can get along without them, especially toward the end of the month." Finally, supervisors could not always predict which month's budget would be charged with an expenditure. "When they throw charges in, they don't throw them in until the end of the month. I think I'm going along pretty well and then — bang — they hit me with some charges."

[5] These problems, of course, go beyond the controller's department to the other departments, like industrial engineering, that establish the physical determinants of standards. Nevertheless, even when the controller's responsibility is limited to "dollarizing" physical standards established by other departments, the variances appear on accounting reports and the accounting personnel are the ones principally criticized for unacceptable standards.

Tons or Dollars

In those companies where the products can be measured, at least roughly, in physical units, manufacturing and some sales executives make more use of data expressed in physical units than data measured in dollars. Dollar comparisons are made largely in those situations where there is no other common denominator for comparing production or inventory totals. Dollars are better accepted as a unit of measurement in a nail mill than in a tube mill, in Westinghouse than in General Mills.

One reason for the general preference for physical units appears to be that operating men have to take action in terms of physical variables. Before they can see what a variance implies in terms of administrative correction, they must translate it from dollar terms to physical terms. Thus, most factory department heads prefer to have delay time reported in hours of machine time, yield in per cent, efficiency in terms of tons per machine-hour or man-hour, and so on. In most companies, there was a relatively high relationship between the receptivity of operating personnel to accounting data and the willingness of the accounting department to report data in physical units or to relate them to physical units.

Another reason for this preference is that operating men found it easier to make comparisons in physical units because this eliminated the obscuring effect of price changes. For a similar reason — because variances measure a deviation from a standard which is itself subject to change — they often were more interested in historical trends in actual figures than they were in variances.

It may be argued that unless reports are expressed in dollar terms, operating superintendents and foremen will tend to be output-conscious rather than profit-conscious or cost-conscious. But data in physical units can measure efficiency and cost. If the job of a particular department is to produce a product at the lowest possible cost per ton, and if direct labor costs are the principal costs which the department superintendent controls, then cost consciousness may just as validly be expressed in terms of man-hours per ton as in terms of dollars per ton. It can plausibly be argued, too, that the man-hour figure is in this case a better attention director than the dollar figure.

In those situations where department superintendents were using physical criteria rather than dollar criteria to judge their work, the physical units used were frequently measures of efficiency rather than simply of total production, for example, in machine-paced operations, man-hours per unit of product. In departments where material costs were important, the percentage yield of materials was watched closely.

Operating executives show little resistance to dollar figures in cost comparison studies, where equipment costs have to be balanced against labor costs. In a number of cases — although this is by no means general — a department head or foreman remarked on the usefulness of dollar figures to impress on himself and his men the magnitude of the dollar savings possible through apparently small improvements in yield or productivity. One department head in his meeting with foremen would point out, "That delay cost us one new Chevvy." The comment was also made by several that, "Of course we knew of that loss before the accounting reports came, but it sure strikes home when you put it in dollars instead of pounds of materials."

31

Perhaps the general conclusion to be drawn from these observations is that it is often useful to report to the operating departments both the physical quantities and the dollars — the former as the more effective attention-directing device, the latter as a useful means of increasing cost consciousness. An accounting department that has carefully studied the actual use being made of its data will be in a position to determine the form of its reports that will give them greatest impact.

Reactions to Unacceptable Standards

Now, what occurs when an operating executive is placed in a situation where he fundamentally mistrusts the standards for any of the reasons discussed above, but where his superiors hold him responsible for unfavorable variances and expect explanations from him? There were frequent opportunities to observe how operating men reacted to such situations. The answer was always the same. When the operating man is placed in the position of justifying his performance in terms of a standard that he doesn't regard as fair he has two choices: to change the performance, or to change the measurement of it. And since he regards the measurement of his performance as unfair, he almost inevitably chooses the second alternative. The following two comments are typical of many made during the interviews:

"If you find a variance that's way out, it's either a poor budget or it's not set up properly."

"My boss comes around and asks me about my variance once in a while. This is often a good opportunity to point out things which are wrong with the accounting reports. If I say the standards are off, he should go back and see why the standards are off."

The first reaction of a supervisor who is confronted with an unfavorable variance in an account is to suspect that something has been charged to the account which should not have been charged. Hence, in a situation where the cost accounting is not completely trusted, a great deal of energy of accounting and operating personnel goes into discussion and debate about the correctness of the charges.

The second reaction of the operating man is to look for uncontrollable external circumstances that can explain the unfavorable variance. Thus, in the case of the seasonal item mentioned before, the operating man explains his unfavorable variances by pointing out that they will be balanced by favorable variances the next summer.

Distrust of standards coupled with pressure to eliminate variances leads to preoccupation with "wooden money" savings — to use a term that was current in one factory. When attention is directed by accounting data to an uneconomical operating practice and the practice is corrected, this leads to a real saving for the company that will ultimately be reflected in profits. When the concern with variances is centered on detecting wrong charges and getting these shifted to the proper account, only "wooden money" is saved and company profits are not increased. Here are typical reports by operating men of their use of accounting data to produce "wooden money" savings:

"The foreman keeps a running total of what he has spent. When the report comes back from accounting, he checks his total. It is important to analyze the

32

charges slip by slip. We find that saves us five to six thousand dollars a month on incorrect charges by accounting or some other department."

"There's a good example of another reason why I think these reports are good. If I hadn't had that report, I would never have known this was charged against me."

In the interviews, the relative amount of emphasis on "wooden money" savings proved to be a sensitive index of distrust of standards. In situations where confidence in standards was lowest, the examples given by respondents of their use of accounting data almost all involved reclassification of charges, and not instances where accounting showed opportunities for improving operations.[6]

Participation in Setting Standards

A close relationship was observed between the extent to which variances were used by operating supervisors for attention-directing purposes, and the extent to which they felt they had a voice in setting the standards. This is not to say that accounting records were more accurate, the norms more attainable, and the variables more controllable in companies where operating men helped to set standards. But in these cases, the operating men were more willing to *admit* the accuracy of the records, the attainability of the standards and the controllability of the variables.

In virtually all the companies the responsible operating supervisors participate *formally* in setting up budgets and other standards. In many cases there is even a formal requirement that they attach their signatures to a standard before it becomes effective. From the interviews it appears that these formal requirements are not the important consideration. In several factories certain department heads felt they were under compulsion to accept the goals set for them by the accounting department, the industrial engineering department or higher level management. In these situations they signed — but with mental reservations — and subsequently they showed great interest in achieving "wooden money" savings to meet the standards that they had formally agreed to, but had not really accepted as reasonable.

What are the conditions of "real" participation as distinguished from formal participation? In the two factories where the greatest acceptance of standards was observed, standard-setting was always described as a process of negotiation between superiors and subordinates in the *operating* departments, with the accounting department serving as the recorder of the bargain. The element of judgment, based on intimate knowledge of operating problems, was stressed. The notion that standards could be established objectively by a neutral "umpire" was rejected. A standard was regarded as a cross between a forecast and a promise. It represented a statement of what the operator thought he would achieve and what he was willing to try to achieve.

Two quotations from interviews with department heads in these factories typify the feeling about participation in standard setting. The first was asked: "Do you

[6] This points up the importance of achieving accuracy in accounting charges, and avoiding arbitrary allocations of joint costs. It may not seem to make any difference whether Department A or Department B is charged, and it may seem uneconomical to try to achieve a high degree of accuracy. But the only way to build up trust in accounting, and to encourage its use, is to keep such errors to an absolute minimum. Moreover, the more accurate the original figures, the less time and effort will be spent trying to achieve "wooden money" savings by changes in accounting charges.

have much to say about the standards?" "Oh, yes, I'd say that nine-tenths of the say is really mine, because I'm right down here and can tell what's going on."

Another was asked: "Do you feel that the budget is something that is imposed upon you?" "To some extent we feel that we'd like to have a few more men, but we have to run it like negotiations and try to ask for them."

To avoid misunderstanding, it should be pointed out that real pressure from higher levels of management to improve results was not absent from these situations. The standards that were set were not always "comfortable" ones for the operating man. In fact, he realized that it was his boss's job to operate efficiently and profitably, and that he could only expect to participate in the standard-setting process if he shared that goal.

Official Standards versus Historical Performance

It has been mentioned that higher level executives seldom appeared to use variances from standard as a score card in any mechanical way. Insofar as they used statistical data to judge the over-all performance of subordinates, they were usually chiefly interested in long-term trends. And since standards change periodically, they were often more concerned with the historical trends in actual output, expenditure, or unit cost than they were in the trends in variances.

In one factory, the manager showed a chart of unit costs over the past twenty years — pointing out that improved equipment and operating efficiencies had more than compensated for rising wages and material costs. The production vice president in this company showed us a much-used copy of the same chart. It was evident that this chart represented the real standard that these two men had set for the factory operation. Similarly, in sales departments, sales budgets were usually regarded as derivative goals; the basic aims were expressed in terms of rising sales figures and a constant or increasing share of the market compared with past performances.

The statements of the previous paragraphs apply primarily to companies manufacturing a product that can be measured reasonably well in terms of a simple physical unit — tons of steel, cases of canned goods, tons of flour, feet of wire or pipe, and so on. For these products, historical comparisons of unit processing costs, or of sales, are not too much affected by changes in product mix. In companies like Westinghouse, where dollars provide the only real common denominator for measuring output, dollar standards and variances from standard take on greater importance.

Unofficial Records

Almost every company had some colorful term to describe the unofficial reports kept by operating executives — "black books," "bootleg reports," "butcher books." Invariably, when such records were kept, they showed evidence of constant use. It does not appear that black books create any serious problem of duplication with the accounting system. At least in these companies, the records kept by operating people are of a summary nature, and require very little clerical time for their recording. To the survey team, the significance of the black books was the indication they gave of the kinds of figures first-line supervisors and operating executives found significant and useful. In some cases, accounting figures — for example, monthly figures on dollars per ton — are transcribed from the accounting reports for purposes of handy reference. In other cases, the unofficial records simply amount to a translation of accounting data into physical terms. In still other cases, figures for the black books are taken from the basic production reports originating with the time and production clerks in the factory. By getting data direct from such sources, the operating supervisor had a summary review of operations much sooner than the same data could be received from the controller's department.

KINDS OF PROBLEM-SOLVING USES OF ACCOUNTING DATA

The potential uses of accounting data for problem-solving purposes can be identified by asking what are the important decisions of management policy to which accounting data could be relevant. The list of decisions is generally the same for all companies although the decisions are not made by the same executives or groups of executives in the different companies:

1. *Production cost comparisons.* These are generally problems of choosing efficient ways of making the product. They include questions of —

Plant location.
Elimination or addition of major activities and organization units.
New capital expenditures for equipment, buildings, or the like.
Choice of economical production procedures, including choice of plants in which to produce for a particular order, choice of processes within a plant, and selection of economical materials.

2. *Pricing and product profitability.* These are the problems of setting prices and price policies for shelf goods and special orders, of determining which product lines are profitable, and of developing selective selling policies.

3. *Efficient marketing procedures.* These are problems of allocating sales and advertising expenditures by channels and areas, and evaluating alternative marketing methods.

4. *Inventory policy.* These are the problems of determining the proper size and location of inventories in the light of customer requirements, manufacturing efficiency, costs of holding inventories, speculative risks, and cash requirements.

5. *Labor negotiations.* These are problems of evaluating the effects on costs of pay increases and other issues arising out of contract negotiations.

Perhaps other areas could be added, but most of the operating decisions we encountered where accounting data might be relevant fell under one of these general heads. We have purposely omitted from the list decisions that are primarily questions of accounting procedure, e.g., desirability of placing inventory on a LIFO basis.

Production cost comparisons. Requests for capital appropriations originating within a factory are handled in the same general way in all the seven companies. Usually, the analysis underlying these decisions involves cooperation of three departments. Typically, the engineering department provides estimates of the cost of the new equipment or project. The industrial engineering department provides estimates (or "standards") of physical productivity for the old and the new equipment. The accounting department "dollarizes" the industrial engineering estimates by applying to them the appropriate wage rates, material prices, and burden rates. When a capital appropriation is approved, the accounting department is responsible for charging expenditures to the appropriation. After installation of the new equipment, the accounting department is usually expected to analyze the savings realized and to compare these with the original estimates. Several instances were observed where the controller's department played much the same role in a plant location study.

Accounting data are sometimes used, but much less universally than in connection with appropriations, in choosing between alternative processes, production schedules, or material specifications. The procedure most often observed is that the operating, industrial engineering, or production control department responsible for the decision, uses data obtained from periodic accounting reports rather than special accounting studies. In one company, for example, the controller's department periodically computes the relative costs of manufacturing the same product in different plants. These costs are used by the production control department in allocating orders to the plants. Whenever significant price or wage changes occur, the controller's department sends revised cost estimates to the production control department.

Choices between alternative production processes, made by operating department heads or foremen, also frequently take into account the standard costs based on industrial engineering standards and incorporated in the cost accounting system. Sometimes the available cost data are used; sometimes the accounting department is asked to make special studies.

Personnel of the controller's office and company accounting department participate in decisions of the same general kind, but they are usually broader in scope. Plant location decisions have already been mentioned. In several of these companies, the question has arisen from time to time as to whether a particular manufacturing division should be expanded, or in other cases eliminated. Such decisions almost always involve special studies in which accounting data play an important role.

Pricing and product profitability. The cost accounting systems of all the companies produce standard product cost data. In the companies manufacturing shelf goods, these data generally flow to a price committee of top executives where they provide one basis for determining price policy. In the companies manufacturing to customer order, the accounting department generally provides the sales department with standard costs on individual orders as a basis for quoting prices to customers. Generally, periodic reports are prepared on the profitability of different product lines. These are furnished to the sales departments, where, as will be noted below, they receive varying amounts of attention.

Efficient marketing procedures. Only a few instances were observed of the use of accounting data to deal with problems of advertising policy, relative effectiveness of different sales methods, and the like.[7] One or two examples were found, *e.g.*, a study of the relative economy of different transportation methods. In general, however, to the extent that these problems are formally analyzed at all, the responsibility

---

[7] As mentioned earlier on p. 17, our observations of the use of accounting in the marketing area is based largely on five companies, excluding the two U. S. Steel subsidiaries.

rests largely with a market research unit in the sales department, and the market research unit depends upon "external" data — trade association statistics, market surveys, economic forecasts, and the like — more than upon the internal accounting data.

Inventory policy. The chief use of accounting data in dealing with inventory problems was in preparing forecasts of cash requirements and cash position. Interviews did not show whether these companies use accounting data to estimate the cost of holding inventories, as a basis for determining order points and the like.

Labor negotiations. In all the companies, the controller's department is called upon at the time of labor negotiations to prepare estimates of the cost effect of wage demands.

FACTORS AFFECTING THE USE OF ACCOUNTING DATA

It is apparent that there are two principal ways in which accounting data may come into the problem-solving processes of the surveyed companies. First, persons faced with a decision, or persons assigned the task of making a special analysis, may turn to the periodic accounting reports for data to help them.

Second, an important policy problem may be the occasion for a request to the controller's department, or the controller's department in collaboration with some other, for special data and analyses directed to the specific problem at hand. Although this was not uniform from company to company, many more instances were observed where data from regular accounting reports were used for problem-solving purposes than instances where cost and other data were specially developed for a particular analysis. Special cost data were most frequently assembled in connection with production cost comparisons and wage cost studies.

Since the distinction just made had important implications for organization, it may be worth clarifying by a specific illustration. One way of making a product profitability study is to take the standard product costs, as they appear in the periodic accounting reports, and compare these with sales prices. It might happen — and frequently does — that although the sales revenue for a particular product does not cover the total cost, the product is made on certain manufacturing facilities that could not be put to another use. Hence, it would be important to compare the sales revenue, not with the total cost, but with the variable cost alone. In most cases such a comparison would require the analyst to go behind the periodic accounting reports and to determine how the total cost figures are built up from their components.

Survey results suggest two general directions in which the controller's department can move in order to increase the usefulness of data for problem-solving purposes. One is to elaborate the periodic accounting reports and refine the classification of accounts, so that these reports will themselves answer more of the questions that arise in dealing with policy problems. The other course is to devote more of the resources of the controller's department or other "staff" units to special analyses that go back to the raw data and build up the specific figures that are needed to answer specific questions. Such special analyses can make use of the techniques of statistics and engineering estimation as well as those of accounting.

These two directions — elaboration of periodic accounting reports versus devel-

37

opment of special analyses — are not, of course, mutually exclusive. In the opinion of the survey team, interview results strongly indicate that further development of staff and facilities for special studies is a more promising direction than the elaboration of periodic accounting reports.

The following example will illustrate factors involved. One of the surveyed companies has developed an elaborate product classification code and the controller's department makes a voluminous monthly report showing the cost of goods sold and income for each product class. The merchandising executives of this company are highly critical of the report, use it very little, and think it is probably a waste of money.

First, they are suspicious of the accuracy of the product costs. They know there are all sorts of complicated problems of joint costing in the company's factories, and they do not trust the standards. They recognize that the "unprofitable" items are carrying a share of overhead costs, and that discontinuing them might very well reduce, rather than increase, company profits. They know, too, that from a merchandising standpoint, it may be important to carry a full line of products even if some are really unprofitable.

In the second place, the product classification, although elaborate, is still too rough for use in connection with many specific problems. Changes in product mix within a class seriously alter the figures. The sales executives find it more useful to pick out a few important items in each product class and to use the sales of these items as indices, than to have data that are merely dollar averages of the whole product mix. In this instance it seems probable that the money spent to prepare this elaborate report could be used more effectively for special studies on a statistical basis of particular products and sales problems.

The problems encountered in this case are characteristic and may be generalized:

1. Operating executives are acutely aware of the distinction between fixed and variable costs, and have little patience with average cost data that combine the two categories. Moreover, they usually are aware that a cost which is "fixed" with respect to one decision may be "variable" with respect to another, and that no general-purpose accounting classification will serve their needs for special analyses. For example, manufacturing executives frequently objected to budget standards that penalized them for using "high-cost" equipment. They pointed out that, in a period of near-capacity operation, it was usually highly profitable to increase production even if this required the use of the higher-cost equipment. They felt that the budget should allow for this.[8]

2. The accuracy of standard costs as a measure of *average* costs raises a second problem. The level of accuracy required if standard cost data are to be used for problem-solving purposes is higher than that required for the attention-directing use of accounting data. When operating executives use variances as an attention-directing tool, they are not disturbed if sometimes the accounting standards turn

[8] It should not be impossible in setting the budget to make a distinction between what might be efficient operating practice under near-capacity conditions, and what might be efficient when the plant was operating well below capacity. Perhaps it will be argued that it would complicate the accounting system beyond reason to try to incorporate such factors in it. This may be so. The survey team can only report that in factories where the standard cost system was inflexible in this respect, the result was to decrease the use of accounting data for operating decisions. Use of variable budgets might well resolve such a problem.

out to be wrong, rather than the operating practice. When standard costs are used for pricing decisions or other policy problems, however, the consequences of inaccurate standards are more serious.

3. Operating executives frequently express a dislike for having voluminous periodic accounting reports sent to them each month, when their actual need is for *particular* items of information at a *particular* time. Moreover, elaborate accounting reports make the controller's department vulnerable to the charge that it is wasting money which the operating departments are able to save through improved operations. However groundless the charge may be in a particular instance, *the controller must be sensitive to the real possibility that voluminous reports will produce this reaction* and will damage working relationships between his department and the operating departments. This reaction was encountered frequently enough to indicate that it constitutes a real problem for the controller's department.

These are the reasons for the conclusion that further progress toward problem-solving uses of accounting information will come largely through the development of facilities for special studies. A controller's department that is well organized to provide periodic reports is not necessarily well organized to make special one-shot studies. This organizational problem will be discussed further in the next chapter.

CENTRALIZATION AND DECENTRALIZATION OF ACCOUNTS

What are the implications of survey data for the first aspect of decentralization — the decentralization of the account and report structure? There has been a great deal of discussion, in recent years, of the decentralization of accounts through the preparation of profit and loss statements, and even of balance sheets, for divisions within a company.[9] A more modest, but much more widely adopted, proposal has been the idea of "responsibility accounting" — the idea that accounting reports should be designed to show the costs actually incurred by each administrative unit, preferably down to the responsibility of the individual foreman. These alternatives will be discussed, giving particular attention to the relation of decentralization of accounts to the structure of the company operating organization.

Decentralization of Accounts and Company Organization Structure

To see how the company organization structure affects the desirability of decentralization of accounts, three schematic organization plans will be considered. These illustrate the main types of company organization encountered in the survey:

Type A. A company organized on the basis of a number of relatively independent operating divisions, each manufacturing and selling its own group of products, and selling most of its products to outside customers, rather than to

[9] See Perrin Stryker, "P & C for Profit," *Fortune,* April 1952, for a recent example of such discussion. The duPont organization is generally credited with the earliest large application of "rate of return on investment" to divisions and departments within the corporation. For their method see, *How the duPont Organization Appraises Its Performance,* American Management Association, Financial Management Series, Number 94, New York: American Management Association, 1950.

other divisions of the company. Westinghouse came closest to this scheme of organization.

Type B. A company having a manufacturing department which supervises a number of factories, and a sales department supervising a number of regional and district sales offices. Eastman Kodak, H. J. Heinz, General Mills (Food Division), and the two U. S. Steel subsidiaries follow this general pattern.

Type C. A company organized into a manufacturing department supervising a number of factories, and a sales department which supervises a number of retail stores. National Supply falls in this category, although only a portion of the sales are made through company-operated stores, and a substantial part of the goods sold by these branches are purchased from other companies.

The three principal technical problems that arise in the construction of decentralized accounts are:

The allocation of indirect costs and overhead to the decentralized units.
The determination of the costs and prices to be used in the interunit transfer of inventories, and
The basis for crediting sales to particular sales offices.

The closer the organization approaches Type A, the less serious these problems are; for in Type A, each division of the organization is relatively self-contained and, except for the allocation of company overhead, problems of interunit transfer and allocation are at a minimum. For organizations of Types B and C, all three problems are likely to be severe. Consider first the question of decentralized profit and loss statements, and then the other forms of decentralized account structures.

Decentralized Profit and Loss Statements

Preparing formal periodic profit and loss statements for particular operating units — factories or retail branches, for example — is subject to one difficulty of a most fundamental kind. Whenever there is much interdependence between units, *e.g.,* one set of units sells the product that is manufactured by another set of units, allocating of costs and receipts between them becomes a highly arbitrary procedure. No amount of refinement in the accounting methods used for allocation can eliminate the fact of interdependence. As a result, there is no reason to suppose that there will be a close correlation between increases or decreases of profits for individual units, and increases or decreases of profits for the company as a whole. Some examples will clarify the problems which come to mind.

When manufactured goods are charged to the sales department or consigned to company-operated stores, what rate of profit should be added to the standard cost of manufacture? Or should the imputed price be based on the open market price at which the sales department could purchase the products outside? The question answers itself *if* the sales department is really permitted to buy outside when this is cheaper, and *if* the manufacturing department has full control over its prices. But few companies leave such departments entirely free in these respects. If, on the contrary, there are reasons why one division should buy from another, even at a higher cost, or reasons why the manufacturing department should not set its own prices, then some part of the profit of the using or selling division ought to be allocable to the manufacturing operation. That is, under these circumstances, it would be logical to credit the manufacturing department at a price higher than the market price.

The converse question, which raises the same issues, is — should the rate of profit allowed the manufacturing department on products consigned to company-operated stores be the same as the average rate earned on direct sales to customers? There is another question whose answer appears obvious, but isn't — should the manufacturing department be credited with goods produced at the actual or standard cost of manufacture? If the former alternative is taken, a manufacturing profit and loss statement makes no sense. But to take the latter alternative is to assume that cost standards are sufficiently accurate so that cost variances really represent manufacturing inefficiencies. We found few factory executives who were willing to grant this assumption.

Where sales are made to the home office of a company with geographically decentralized operations, and with delivery to a number of locations, should the sales be credited to the sales district where the customer's home office lies, or to the district where delivery is made? Practical tax and administrative considerations often require that the latter alternative be adopted. This, regardless of whether it leads to a rational accounting for profits. Should company overhead be allocated to the divisions at actual or standard? If the latter, how should unabsorbed or over-absorbed burden be handled? In either case, what should be the basis for allocation? The list of questions can be extended indefinitely.

To sum up, where the activities of two or more divisions of a company are in fact highly interdependent, it is very difficult to allocate total company profits among the divisions in a rational, precise manner. Under these circumstances, it becomes questionable as to how much weight can be placed upon these divisional "profits" in determining the effectiveness of the divisional executives. However convenient it would be for top management to have a single profit figure to summarize divisional performance to serve as a divisional incentive, it may turn out that such a simple but unrealistic criterion is less helpful than the more subjective but realistic bases which are commonly used for judging divisional management.

These problems are all familiar ones to any company controller, and especially to one who has experimented with decentralized profit and loss accounting. It is not the purpose of this study to elaborate on arguments from economic and accounting theory. Rather, it is to see whether information obtained from operating executives gives any indication of the effect of decentralized profit and loss accounting on actual use made of accounting data for score-card, attention-directing, and problem-solving purposes.

The notion often expressed, that formal profit and loss statements are useful and necessary to stimulate "profit consciousness," appeared to be largely unfounded. A high level of profit consciousness was observed among executives at all levels. There was no lack of understanding that profit is the final score for the company as a whole. But for his own score card, each operating executive generally wanted data that would indicate *the effect of his own operations* on profits. With a few exceptions, a profit and loss statement was not regarded as the most effective report for this purpose. The exceptions were primarily managers of relatively self-contained divisions — men responsible for both manufacturing and sales functions.

Executives were not *un*interested in learning about their profit performance, but the profit and loss statements were not considered important management tools. Where factories or departments were highly interdependent, and the "profits" recorded on paper were affected by accounting methods, the general tendency was to complain about the accounting procedures when profits were low, rather than to assume that the operations needed improvement. The "profits" were not accepted as a valid operating standard.

Any gain from letting executives know about the profits of decentralized units can probably also be achieved by letting them know, from time to time, what spread has to be maintained between their costs and selling prices to secure a satisfactory company profit. Managers were frequently found applying such rules of thumb: "We will do all right if we can keep the manufacturing cost down to X% of the sales price." Executives operating in this way did not appear to be less profit-conscious in their management than those who had formal profit figures.

In interpreting these findings, one caution needs to be noted. The survey team was in a position to observe the extent to which operating executives were or were not profit-conscious at the time of the survey. It was also possible to observe how they reacted to profit and loss statements, and what use they made of them. Obviously, it is impossible to observe and to forecast whether regular presentation to executives of profit and loss statements would bring about any change over a long period of years — ten or fifteen — in their attitudes toward profits. There was no evidence of any cumulative effect in this direction resulting from past practices in these companies, but almost none of them had used decentralized profit and loss statements for more than about five years. One company had abandoned them after some years of experience, for reasons similar to those that have been presented here. But controllers in several other companies felt that they had observed some increased profit-consciousness among operating executives since the introduction of decentralized profit and loss statements.

The survey team's general conclusion is that the increase in attention to profits is to be attributed largely to factors other than the one in question here, since it does not appear to be confined to companies with decentralized profit and loss statements. Among these other factors, which have been important in the decade preceding this study, are:

The trend from a seller's to a buyer's market after World War II — particularly around 1949.

The increase in the proportion of college-trained operating executives, who are oriented less exclusively toward production or sales volume than were executives of an earlier generation.

The growing use of special analyses to determine the effect on profit of proposed manufacturing or sales policies.

The growing use of various kinds of decentralized accounting statements — *not necessarily in the form of profit and loss statements.*

The third of these factors was treated at length in pages 35 to 37 of this chapter, and the fourth factor will be discussed in the remainder of the chapter.

42

Responsibility Accounting

From previous discussion of the attention-directing uses of data, what appears to be important is *to establish decentralized reporting for expenditure and income items that the operating executive can control.* There are four main reasons for avoiding overelaboration of the decentralized accounting reports. First, since there is nothing the executive or supervisor can or will do about the uncontrollable items, it is an unnecessary expense. Second, it makes the reports difficult to understand, and discourages operating men from using those portions of the report which they can understand and do something about. Third, it leads to resentment, because it is believed that top management is using an unreliable score card to judge the results of subordinates. Fourth, it frequently leads to delays in getting reports into the hands of operating executives and supervisors. When reports were too elaborate, the reactions were almost uniformly of the following kind:

"One of the big troubles with these statements is that there are too many things in the reports that we can't control and have nothing to do with. Some of these items just make the reports more difficult to read and harder to understand. Then we keep getting 'red' variances on these uncontrollable items."

"Well, as long as you can explain the variances, it's all right, isn't it?"

"No, it really isn't. My foremen feel that even though they can explain, they are held accountable for them. These reports I'm sure are summarized when they are sent to the home office, and I'm sure those men are too busy to look down and analyze everything on them, so they probably judge us by the total. Therefore, we're being criticized unduly for things that are not our fault at all."

When company overhead is allocated to the plants and reported on the monthly statements, these statements cannot be prepared until the home office has provided the overhead data. In practice, this almost always results in a substantial delay in the reports. In one company, a partial report, excluding overhead charges, was provided to the factories shortly after the close of the reporting period. A final report, more complete and accurate, followed several weeks later. The prompt, incomplete reports were used a great deal; the complete reports almost not at all. Much evidence of the same kind was observed in the other companies.

Conclusions

Survey observations seem to support the general conclusion that a formal divisional profit and loss statement probably justifies the cost of preparing it only where the company is so organized that a "division" is a highly self-contained administrative unit, manufacturing and selling a well-defined product or group of products in relative independence from other units in the company. Where this condition is not satisfied, the benefits claimed for decentralized profit and loss accounting can largely be attained more economically with less radical forms of responsibility accounting.

What general rule does this suggest for the design of a decentralized accounting system? First, the accounting classification by responsibilities should be sufficiently refined to permit preparation of cost statements for individual foremen, branch managers, and higher levels of operating management. Second, only those costs should be reported at each level which are controllable, at least to some degree, by the responsible supervisor or executive. In a factory, for example, this would generally include direct labor costs, material variances due to yield, operating supplies and tools, as well as repairs and maintenance charges. General factory overhead, material costs other than yield variances, and similar items are best excluded. At best, repairs and maintenance charges will always cause problems because of the divided responsibility. Such problems can be minimized by a procedure which requires the signature of individual foremen to authorize the charges.

Chapter 4

ORGANIZATION FOR CONTROLLERSHIP SERVICE: CENTRALIZATION, DECENTRALIZATION

Having surveyed and reviewed significant factors determining how accounting data are used, conclusions can be developed about controllership and accounting organization, and the effects of varying degrees of centralization or decentralization of accounting activities, and correlative factors of authority, loyalties, and communications.

Summary

This chapter discusses the organization of the controller's department and the effects on use of accounting data with reference to basic, company-wide problems and problems common to several divisions or departments of the company. In the following chapter, those aspects will be discussed which apply specifically to factory and to sales accounting.

Major topics discussed in this chapter are:

Organizing to encourage attention-directing use of accounting data.
Organizing to increase problem-solving use of accounting data.
Organizing record-keeping functions.
The internal organization of the controller's department for simultaneous pursuit of the above objectives.
The over-all organization of company (headquarters) accounting functions.

So far as current analysis and special studies are concerned, the important aspect of centralization and decentralization is to develop effective channels of *communication* at the proper levels between personnel of the controller's department and personnel of the operating departments. There are no large cost differences in organizing these particular functions in one way or another. Hence, the principal applicable criterion of effectiveness is the *quality of the informational service* provided by the controller's department to the operating departments. With respect to the record-keeping and periodic reporting functions discussed in pages 60 to 66, however, the geographical location of accounting units is the principal aspect of centralization and decentralization which is involved.

ORGANIZING FOR ATTENTION DIRECTING: CURRENT ANALYSIS

Inducing Use of Accounting Data and Services

Survey results indicate that there is no one best way for getting executives into the habit of comparing their performance with standards and determining the causes for the deviations. However, an essential condition for attention-directing use of data is that accounting reports be reviewed periodically, in order to determine when performance is "off standard" and to initiate inquiries as to the reasons. It was found, for example, that factory department heads in seven of the nine surveyed factories make considerable use of accounting data. Yet there is no single factor common to all these factories which distinguishes them sufficiently from the other two, to explain the difference in utilization of data. Actually, interview results show that accounting data are used if any *one* of the following three types of conditions is satisfied:

Data are used when the executive is convinced they help him do his job. But he may use them for different reasons — to improve his own operation, or in supervising his subordinates. There were several striking instances of men who use data extensively, even in plants where the general level of use is low. These exceptional men either have better-than-average ability to use and comprehend data, or they have at some time in their careers had some accounting experience.

Data are used when the operating executive sees that "success" in his job, as viewed by the company, depends upon an evaluation made in terms of the accounting records. There are two main variations of this situation. First, the operating executive may want to earn a bonus which is directly or indirectly tied into the accounting system. In these instances, as noted in the previous chapter, there is frequently an excessive preoccupation with reclassification of costs, the correction of errors, and with "wooden money" savings — rather than with the use of data to improve operations. Second, the operating executive uses his accounting data when he knows that his superior is going to pay attention to the same data, and will expect him to explain off-standard performance. This procedure is effective when explanations are called for regularly, and when superficial explanations are not acceptable.

Data are used when the operating man is systematically helped or forced to pay attention to his reports. This attention-directing by an outside party may be done either through a staff assistant or through a collaborative arrangement with an accounting man — the operating executive may have a staff assistant, one of whose primary duties is to analyze reports and call unusual items to his attention. In this case, so long as the assistant thinks of data analysis as an important part of his job, it matters little whether his boss has strong feelings toward the use of accounting data. The establishment of the job of assistant "institutionalizes" attention to the data.

Sometimes an accounting man is given responsibility for producing, in cooperation with the operating men, a formal written explanation of the variances in the daily, weekly, or monthly cost statement. This procedure appears to be effective when the accounting reports are reasonably prompt.

However, both of these devices transfer the motivation from the operating executive to another person — to the staff assistant or to the accounting man. Unless someone at a higher level reviews and controls the quality of the variance explanation, the attention-directing may become a superficial formality.

In view of these and other ways for bringing about the use of available accounting data, it might appear that there are no serious organization problems here. But this would assume a utopia where all operating executives possess all the

46

qualities executives *should* have and where accounting data are so constituted that they automatically induce use by operating executives. Actually, of course, the controller must often begin with a state of affairs in which accounting data are not used very effectively. His problem then is to bring about enough understanding of data and of operating executives' needs for data so that the operating executives will *want* to use the data — and so that the value of the data will be demonstrated by such use. The organizational problem is to find ways whereby the controller's department can encourage the use of, interest in, and understanding of accounting data. Effective two-way communication is, thus, of prime importance.

The less the operating men are self-motivated to use accounting data, the more the controller's department must take active steps to remedy the situation. The two directions in which the controller can move to expand and improve use of accounting services are related to the second and third of the sources of motivation described above.

One way in which the controller's department can take the initiative is to do a more effective job of funneling upward reports from factories and sales units and bringing them to the attention of the president, vice presidents for manufacturing and sales, and so on. As the other executives in the company offices begin to discover how such accounting reports can help *them* in working with their own subordinates, these subordinates in the ranks of middle management will be called upon more and more to interpret and explain the reports to their superiors. As executives in middle management begin to recognize that the accounting reports are part of the basis upon which their work is reviewed, they will look for ways to become better informed.

The second way in which the controller's department can take the initiative is to get top management endorsement for a regular, systematic interpretation of monthly cost variances, to be prepared by operating men with the assistance of analysts from the factory accounting department. This procedure will prepare the way for a regular and growing contact between the controller's department and operating men at middle management levels.

Once efforts along these lines have induced some desire for accounting service and information on the part of the operating men, the controller's department can direct more of its effort to further improvement of the accounting data, reports, and service. In this way the use of these services "pays off" more directly and richly for the operating executive; the executive himself becomes convinced that the data help him, and he sees that his success in the eyes of his superiors will be enhanced by intelligent use of the data.

Providing Channels for Flow of Accounting Information

Critical to the whole process of attention-directing is the centralization and decentralization of communications — the channels through which accounting information flows. In particular, there must be both "horizontal" channels through which accounting contacts are made, permitting a flow between the controller's department and the operating organization, and "vertical" channels permitting a flow between levels of the operating organization. Through careful attention to the

47

design and operation of these channels, the controller's department can take steps to secure effective utilization of its services.

The general relationships of the communications channels under discussion are depicted on the accompanying chart (Figure 1):

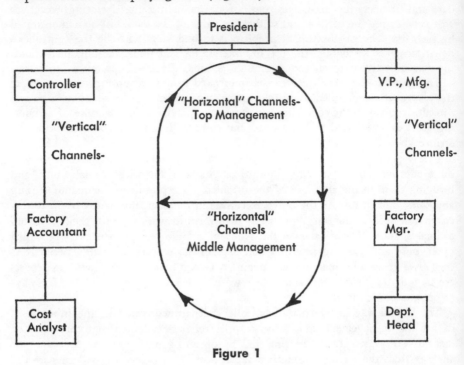

Figure 1

"HORIZONTAL" AND "VERTICAL" CHANNELS OF COMMUNICATION

This chart illustrates the "horizontal" channels between controller's department and operating departments at top-management and middle-management level. It shows how information, fed upward through accounting channels and across through horizontal channels at top level, can be fed downward again through operating "vertical" channels to induce greater middle-management attention to accounting data.

"Horizontal" Communications Channels

A "horizontal" channel of contact provides for direct communication of the accounting personnel and corresponding operating people at approximately the same level within the organization. For example, an accounting manager or an office manager in a regional or district sales office would provide such a channel with the regional or district sales manager; a factory accountant with a factory manager. In a large factory, a cost analyst might be assigned to each operating department head; in a smaller factory, one or two analysts might have the responsibility for maintaining contacts wth all the department heads. In the latter case, it may be argued that the channel is not exactly "horizontal." [1]

Functions of horizontal channels. Horizontal communication channels between operating units and the controller's department can and do perform two main functions. First, when the controller's department has all or part of the responsibility for explaining variances, it is through these channels that the accounting personnel get the necessary operating information and discuss problems with the operating executives. Second, through these channels the operating executives can raise questions about the correctness of charges and can initiate requests for changes in standards.

Need for horizontal channels. When the operating executives are strongly motivated to use accounting information, effective horizontal contacts with the controller's department tend to develop spontaneously and at the initiative of the operating departments. The operating men soon learn where to go in the controller's department to get the information they want — and they go there. Through these informal processes, a workable and effective organization develops with little need for formal planning or for elaborate formal procedures. This was true without exception in situations observed where the operating management really wanted to use accounting services. In such cases if formal procedures had been spelled out, they were generally little more than ratifications of informal understandings. And where the formal channels did not provide for direct horizontal contact, these channels were quite freely ignored, used after the fact (to "ratify" informal agreements), or used only when informal agreement could not be reached.

When the operating executives are not strongly motivated to use accounting information, horizontal channels tend to develop only to the extent that they are formally established by the controller's department with support from the chief executive, and to the extent that their use is enforced by assigning to accounting personnel tasks whose completion requires regular contacts with the operating personnel and specific allocation of sufficient manpower and time so that these tasks receive high priority.

If, at the outset, there is very little contact between the controller's department and operating executives, the latter may have little respect or use for accounting information, and may respond without enthusiasm to attempts of accountants to work with them. As a result of the reaction they get from operating people, the accountants may gradually "keep busy" at their own desks to avoid unpleasant or frustrating experiences with operating people. Then communication between the two groups may become less frequent resulting in minimal use of accounting data by operating department heads.

On the other hand, if a definite program is set up, involving regular assignments for accounting personnel requiring them to contact operating supervisors for information, the accountants may begin to arouse the interest of the operating executives in possible uses of accounting data. They may also obtain a better understanding of these executives' needs for data. When this occurs, the operating heads will generally encourage or seek out more frequent contacts with the accountants. Each begins to gain a more thorough understanding of the vocabulary, problems

[1] See pp. 51 and 55 for a discussion of the question whether it is important to have a strict one-to-one relationship between accounting personnel and operating units.

and methods of the other. This cycle continues until a fairly high degree of communication and use of accounting data is attained. The survey team has learned of examples of both developments and has observed both high level and low level equilibrium in relationships between the controller's department and factory department heads.

A common first reaction, when regular contacts are established between the controller's and operating departments, is that the operating supervisors view these contacts as opportunities to unload their "gripes" about the accounting system, to complain about incorrect charges and unreasonable standards. Despite comments about "wooden money" savings, the effort that is spent in meeting these complaints, demands, and requests is not wasted. *They provide the controller's department with an opportunity to show that it really intends to* provide data in useful and usable form, in terms of operating departments' needs so that when it is asked for help, it meets such requests promptly. Finally, it helps to sell operating men on the reasonableness of standards if the controller's department will accept correction when it makes mistakes and if it pays attention to criticism of its procedures and standards.

What happens if the controller's department does *not* seize opportunities to provide prompt service when requests are made by operating men? This was illustrated in the two factories where the least use was being made of accounting information. In these two factories the response to requests for review of standards was frequently so tardy and grudging that the operating men were discouraged from renewing them. We heard complaints like this:

"The standards haven't been adjusted. It takes quite a while. They have to look at it for a year and by the time they get around to it, I guess it would take two or three years to get them changed right."

The accounting personnel in these particular factories failed to realize that when a matter was important enough to an operating executive for him to inquire about it, this was sufficient reason for giving the inquiry prompt and serious attention, even though it might seem trivial or stupid to the controller's department. The importance of such an inquiry lies not so much in its content as in the opportunity it provides to give concrete evidence that the controller's department is really willing to work with the operating executives and departments. This lack of understanding was reflected in the following comment by the factory controller in one of these two situations:

"In cost reporting we have tried to explain the system to the factory manager for some time. We might as well not bother. He has his mind set on what he wants."

"Why don't you give him what he wants?"

"Well, the type of reports we make out are prepared for the company accounting department."

"Why not make two sets — one for him, and one for the company office?"

"I see no reason why we couldn't, but after all, the company has already decided what is best and what should be suitable for the job. The data are sufficient to handle his needs. I use the same cost figures, and I get all I want."

Effectiveness of channels. There are a number of other factors which appeared to make for more or less effective horizontal communication, although the one just discussed — providing regular occasions for contact — is perhaps the most important. These other factors include: the extent to which operating executives understand the accounting system, the extent to which the accounting contact men understand operations, how close the office or desk of the accountant is to the operating department, and the relative status of the accounting and operating men who deal with each other.

Mutual understanding of accounting and operating problems. Decentralized communication — direct contact between accountants and operating executives — is one of the principal ways in which the operating man learns to use accounting data and the accountant learns about operating technology and problems. Conversely, as this mutual understanding increases, it becomes easier to keep each in frequent contact with the other. The survey findings, however, do not indicate that formal training programs in themselves have been particularly effective in bringing about such understanding. In a number of cases when a new cost system was installed, a series of meetings was held to acquaint supervisors and foremen with the system. Such meetings were probably not without value. However, it is quite clear that, when other elements of an effective relationship were absent, training sessions were not sufficient by themselves to produce it. The most effective instances of formal training programs were meetings held by operating executives for their subordinates and focused on the periodic review of cost and operating statements.

The magnitude of the two-way educational job to be done can not be overestimated. Even in situations where most use was being made of accounting information, there were numerous admissions by operating men that they did not understand the accounting system, and numerous complaints that the accountants did not understand operations. Similarly, accounting personnel were often reasonably free in admitting they did not know too much about operations and even freer in complaining that operating men did not understand the accounting system. Even where decentralized communications patterns had been established, there was room for increased understanding. The survey facts suggest that controllers' departments could profitably devote more effort to training their own personnel to understand operations. In this way the controllers' departments could demonstrate their willingness to go half way, or more, in communicating on a working basis, with operating personnel. Operating departments, moreover, must shoulder primary responsibility for training operating men in accounting.

Effects of physical location. The effects of geographical centralization and decentralization upon communications can be discussed quite briefly. All evidence indicates that frequent face-to-face contact is essential for effective communication. In the extreme case where an accounting man is located in a different city from the operating unit with which he is supposed to work, it is almost impossible to achieve a close working relationship. Several such instances were observed in this study. The operating man may still make considerable use of the periodic accounting reports, but he will not form the habit of turning frequently to the controller's department for supplementary analyses, and he will usually encounter difficulties in getting the controller's department to adapt its reports to his specific needs. Where the two are in the same office building, or the same factory, the matter of physical location is of somewhat less importance — although not insignificant. Provided that the accounting man's work assignments give him frequent and regu-

51

lar occasions to get out into the factory or to talk to the operating man in the latter's office, it is not absolutely essential for effective relationships that their offices be close together. On the other hand, where it is feasible, bringing offices together is one of the simplest administrative devices available for encouraging frequent contact.

Status relationships. Status relationships also affect the communication pattern. In horizontal communication the operating man generally has a higher administrative position and status than the accounting man with whom he deals. The district sales manager normally deals with the office manager, the factory manager with the factory chief accountant, and so on. It helps reduce fears of operating personnel that the controller's department may exercise "authority" over them. However, it may make the accountant's job more difficult, for it leaves with the operating man the greater initiative in determining how much accounting service he will demand or accept. This is one reason why it appears so important that the activities of the controller's department receive real support from the operating executives at higher levels.

On the other hand, when the difference between the status of the accounting man and the operating man is more than one or two levels in the administrative hierarchy, the initiative in the relationship is more one-sided. Such a relationship seemed to be satisfactory when operating executives already had strong motivations for using accounting service (and hence were willing to take the initiative in the relationship), but much less satisfactory for developing such services where they did not already exist.

"Vertical" Communications Channels

The most important "vertical" channel in the matter of attention-directing is the direct relationship between an operating executive and his immediate subordinates, or his immediate superior. The use of that channel has been described in some detail in Chapter 3, pages 23 to 24 and 27 to 28. It appears that a sure-fire way of securing the extensive use of accounting data by executives at a particular level (say, factory department heads) is to make certain that the executive immediately above them calls on them frequently and regularly for explanations of off-standard performance. Where this was done, the impact of reports was felt at least one, and usually two, stages downward in the operating chain of command.

When the company production executives required a monthly explanation of variances from the factory manager, and when they demonstrated their concern with the report by frequent comments on it, the factory manager almost invariably was using the same practice with his department heads, and the department heads with their foremen. In these companies it was common practice for the factory manager to hold monthly (or more frequent) cost meetings with his department heads, and for the department heads to hold weekly or bi-weekly meetings with foremen. The same thing was observed in the sales area.

Moreover, company executives exert considerable influence over which reports and standards of performance receive the most attention at other levels of the hierarchy as a result of the way these vertical channels are used. Some survey observations on this point are of considerable interest in showing how organization affects the use of accounting data.

52

In one factory, the manager holds periodic meetings with his department heads to review, department by department, how they are making out on their production quotas. Although this factory has a rather complete cost accounting system, the factory manager reviews the cost reports with his subordinates less systematically and less completely than the production reports. This attitude is reflected in almost every department, where great attention is paid to reaching production quotas, but where the interest in cost variances is relatively low.

In the U. S. Steel Company, the controller's department prepares for company-wide "committees on practice" reports on blast furnace operations, open hearth operations, and so on, comparing operating results for all the works having those facilities. The "practice reports" receive careful attention from department heads, and their relative standing with competitive facilities at other works is one of the performance yardsticks that they watch most closely. These reports are not "dollarized" reports, but they include measures both of output and efficiency, stated mostly in physical units.

In the Westinghouse Electric Corporation, several of the operating vice presidents have on their staffs assistants who keep a continuing check on particular items — especially items that constitute current problems with which top management is concerned. Factory management, including general and section foremen, is clearly aware that these items are receiving top-level attention, and the items become important as performance measures.

In all these companies, by following up closely on particular performance items, top management quickly secures special attention to these items by management at lower levels. This is evidently a management tool of great power, and one that needs to be used with special care. For if too much emphasis is placed upon particular items, the operating management may concentrate upon making a "score" on these items, and may pay less attention than is desirable to others. To cite an obvious example, when there is too much top management pressure for "tonnage," unit costs may suffer — and vice versa. The controller's department, in the efforts it exerts to secure effective use of data, can have a substantial influence on the relative attention that is paid to volume, unit costs, and other items that affect the over-all profit picture.

Communications: Some Implications for Organization

It appears that the development of effective horizontal and vertical channels of communication is of crucial importance for the attention-directing uses of accounting data. Only in exceptional cases can the self-motivation of operating executives be relied upon completely for this purpose. To reinforce this motivation, the controller's department can use horizontal channels to encourage the regular examination of deviations from performance standards, and higher-level operating executives can use vertical channels for the same purpose.

Organization when use of reports is adequate. Where adequate attention to data is secured through self-motivation and the use of vertical channels, the controller's department can concentrate on providing effective information service, and need not be unduly concerned with "selling" the service it provides. In this case one function of decentralized horizontal channels is to inform the controller's department about improvements needed in its reports, and need for review or changes in standards or in standard determinants. The channels also should give the operating executives a means for obtaining supplementary information in explanation of reports, and a means for correcting errors in charges and other accounting mistakes.

Under these circumstances operating executives can be counted on to work through the channels they find effective. Hence, formal organization tends to be of secondary importance. What is chiefly required of the controller's department is that it be adequately staffed and trained to handle the requests it receives.

Organization to encourage use of reports. Where the controller's department believes that inadequate use is made of its reports, and wishes to improve on the situation, communications channels take on additional strategic importance. Every care must be taken to establish frequent and direct contact with operating executives, and to establish it at the proper points of the operating organization.

Several steps can be taken to encourage frequent and regular communication. These steps have already been suggested, and require only brief statement:

1. Give controller's department personnel definite assignments which require working with operating men. The simplest device of this kind is to require accounting personnel, with the cooperation of operating men, to prepare explanations of variances from performance standards.

2. Give these assignments high priority. Insure that they will not be neglected under the pressure of report deadlines or other duties.

3. Locate the controller's staff man as close as possible to his counterpart in the operating department.

4. Place contact responsibilities at a high enough level in the controller's department so that the gap in status between this man and his counterpart in operation will not be too great.

5. In every possible way, try to staff contact positions with personnel who have a thorough understanding of operations.

The important levels of the operating organization with which horizontal communications need to be established depend very much on the organization of each particular company. Nevertheless, criteria can be applied:

> If meaningful explanations of variances are to be prepared, they can only be obtained from persons close to operations. This means that there must be direct contact with operating executives or supervisors who actually observe operations at first hand — usually factory department supervisors or sales district supervisors.
>
> So that horizontal channels can be reinforced by the vertical communication channels, the controller's department must encourage and assist top production and sales executives of the company to discuss with their subordinates problems indicated by accounting reports and explanations of variances.
>
> The most important area of production and sales management between top management and the front line of operations will be those production and sales executives with responsibility to "run their own shows" under very general direction. This usually means the executive

responsible for an individual factory, regional or district sales operation. In a very large company with semi-autonomous divisions, for example, Westinghouse and General Mills, the division probably represents the most important intermediate stage of management.

In the initial stages, the controller's department should concentrate on developing effective communications at three principal levels of the operating organization to get increased use of accounting data. In many large companies there may be additional levels between the production vice president and the factory manager, between the factory manager and the first-line manager, and between the general sales manager and the regional or district sales manager. Survey results do not indicate a need for the controller's department to parallel each level in the operating organization with a level in its own organization — or that there is anything to be gained by such an elaboration of the accounting organization.

For example, a company where the sales department was subdivided by principal product lines, it was possible for the same accounting personnel to maintain contacts with the general sales manager and with his principal subordinates. In a company with geographically decentralized production districts, each responsible for the factories in its area, effective contact with the home office production executives and with the factory managers appeared to obviate the need for direct accounting assistance to the district executives. Indeed, the factory budget procedure appeared to work more effectively when there was direct contact between the factory and the home office, by-passing the district office.

Method of preparing explanations of variances. Responsibility for preparing analyses of variances from performance standards can be placed solely in the controller's department, solely in the operating departments, or can be shared between them. Almost the whole range of these possibilities was observed in this survey.

The organizational question is not so much to decide which is desirable as to decide which is possible. To initiate the practice of writing explanations of variances, the controller's department may have to assume the primary responsibility at the outset. Later, with good working relationships established between the controller's department and operating departments, it may be possible to transfer the responsibility to the operating departments.

Our observations indicate that it is clearly unsatisfactory for the accounting department to accept responsibility for preparing the variance explanations without making certain that the explanations are receiving attention from top or key operating executives, and are used by these executives in their contacts with subordinates.

In addition, the evidence suggests the following procedures in cases where a considerable part of the responsibility for explaining variances rests with the accounting department. First, the explanations should probably be transmitted upward through accounting channels rather than operating channels. But the operating executive whose department is concerned should know what is in the reports. Second, top-ranking personnel in the controller's department should be assigned the definite task of bringing to the attention of responsible operating executives items which they believe should be discussed with operating subordinates. In other words, if the accounting department takes the initiative in the area of variance analysis, it must take steps to strengthen the vertical as well as the horizontal channels of communication.

There are two additional prerequisites to the successful use of variance explanations under any procedure. First, the explanations must be based on an actual knowledge of what is going on in the operating departments. This knowledge can be provided by operating men at a level not higher than the department head (or general foreman where departments are very large), or by an accounting man who has direct contact with these operating men and who gets out frequently into the factory. *Useful* variance explanations cannot be dreamed up in the accounting office under any circumstances.

Second, where the explanations are prepared on a weekly or monthly basis, it is important that someone — either an accounting man or an operating man — keep a current daily log of occurrences that may cause and explain variances. The evidence is conclusive that it is impossible to reconstruct, at the end of a month, a sufficiently detailed account of happenings to trace the true causes of the variances. Where the operating men cannot immediately be induced to keep such a log, the accounting department must perforce assume a greater share of responsibility for providing the explanations.

ORGANIZING FOR PROBLEM SOLVING: SPECIAL STUDIES

Answering the question of how to organize the controller's department for problem-solving uses of data is more difficult than answering the corresponding question for the attention-directing uses of data. Development of the special studies area, and the establishment of groups in the controller's department primarily concerned with this function, are relatively recent trends in controllership. In about half the surveyed companies, definite organization units of one kind or another had been created in the controller's department to conduct special studies. In the other companies, special analyses resulted from specific assignments to personnel who also had other responsibilities — supervision and current analysis.

Historically, accounting organizations were developed with a view primarily to preparing periodic accounting reports, and secondarily to assisting operating management in the interpretation and use of these reports. Because the trend toward analysis is recent, and because controllers are still not in agreement on their responsibilities in this area, conclusions reached today as to appropriate organizational arrangements will need to be re-examined when these trends are better defined a few years hence. Observations made on this survey resulted in findings which bear on three important issues involved in this organizational question:

1. The amount of emphasis placed upon problem-solving studies varied widely in the seven companies. This provided an opportunity to observe what kinds of organizational arrangements appear to make special analysis work possible and effective. In particular, the survey team sought to determine which levels of the operating organization had the greatest need for assistance from the controller's department on special studies, and to observe what channels of communication were effective for providing the service.

2. Analysis of such observations indicates that organization for problem-solving

is not purely an internal matter for the controller's department. It is a company-wide organizational problem which raises questions as to the appropriate relationships among the controller's department, the manufacturing and sales departments, and other "staff" departments such as industrial engineering. The important issues of this problem will be considered, therefore, without resolving the broad question as it affects all these departments.

3. The broadening scope of the controller's functions in some of these companies is slowly bringing about a changing concept of the scope and nature of the accountants' tasks and responsibilities. New and broader skills are required of accountants engaged in analytical work. In most of the surveyed companies, however, the picture most accounting personnel still have of their own function places relatively little stress on special analysis for problem-solving purposes. This appeared to be true even in those companies which have gone furthest with the analytical function. Hence, the organizational question raises problems with respect to the nature of the accounting profession and the training it provides for the controllership function.[2]

Organization Levels for Problem-Solving Service

The organization plan and the staffing plan which would enable the controller's department to do the most effective job in the attention-directing area are not necessarily the most appropriate for problem solving. In particular, the levels of operating management which have the greatest need for the first kind of service are not generally the same as those that need the second. Hence, a different pattern of communications channels may also be called for in the two cases.

Types of major policy problems for which special accounting analyses might be employed are:

Production cost comparisons and alternative facilities.
Prices and product profitability.
Choices of efficient marketing methods.
Desirable inventory levels.
Labor negotiations.

The organization levels at which such problems arise, the levels at which the analysis of the problems are made, and the levels at which the final decisions are made and approved vary from company to company.

The interviews show, insofar as the controller's department is called upon for help in such decisions, that the assistance is sought through horizontal channels of communication. The factory manager looks to the factory accounting executive or one of his principal assistants; the company production manager to the company controller or one of his division heads. Moreover, the stage of problem solving where the data are needed is usually the intermediate stage when some operating executive is charged with the task of investigating the problem and presenting a recommendation for its solution.

The first step, then, in securing greater use of accounting data in problem solving is to identify those points in the organization where this intermediate stage

[2] Discussed in Chapter 6, pp. 98-100.

occurs. The second step is to strengthen the control and accounting organization at these levels.

In these companies, the persons principally involved in actual analytical work are the personal assistants to top executives, and the "staff" departments at company and factory levels. These include industrial engineering and metallurgical departments, production scheduling units, inspection and quality control units, and market research units. It is, therefore, apparent that the channels which the controller's department develops for dealing with operating executives in the area of current analysis will not necessarily be effective for bringing accounting data into the problem-solving process.

Formalizing the decision-making process. With great consistency, the areas in which the controllers' departments were found to be participating most actively in special problems work were areas where the decision-making process had been formalized, and where the controller's department had a formally defined role in the process. The best examples, already described in Chapter 3, were the definite procedures that had been established in most of the companies for justifying proposed capital expenditures and for pricing special orders. These procedures enable the controller's department to learn, at an early stage, what problems are under study, and, therefore, to contribute data and analyses to the decision-making process.

This suggests the possibility of establishing similar procedures in other decision-making areas where they do not now exist. For example, in several of the companies, the market research unit does not regularly consult the controller's department. There are only exceptional requests for specific data. Another device which appears to be useful for bringing the controller's department into the problem-solving process is a formal cost reduction program tied into the operating budgets. The cost reduction program gives operating executives an additional incentive to analyze carefully the economies of possible operating changes, and accounting personnel are likely to be drawn into this process.

Scope of Controller's Department Participation

The discussion of the last section was based on the implicit assumption that it is desirable for the controller's department to play a large rôle in problem-solving and decision-making processes. As was pointed out above, this is really a top management question, since it involves other departments as well as the controller's.

In large organizations, important decisions are almost always group decisions — in the sense that a considerable amount of specialized and expert knowledge is brought to bear on a problem before a decision is reached. No matter where the problem originates, what person or persons have responsibility for investigating it, or what executive makes a final decision, the organization's specialized resources have to be tapped and brought into focus on the problem. What clues can be obtained from an examination of the nature of the decisions themselves which might serve as guidelines in finding an appropriate rôle for the controller's department in the decision-making process?

In the first place, solutions of most of these problems require operating or technical knowledge to a far greater extent than knowledge of accounting or statistical techniques. An example drawn from one of the steel works is typical. When a rolling mill does not crop enough metal from the ends of its billets, the number of imperfections that occur at the next stage of processing increases. If too much metal is cropped, the imperfections decrease, but the rolling mill yield decreases also. Clearly, there is some "right amount" of cropping that just balances the rolling mill yield against the cost of imperfections. If the relationship between the cropping practice and the frequency of imperfections is known, it is a relatively simple task to compute the costs. But estimating the relationship is not at all simple, and is something that requires intimate metallurgical and practical knowledge of the process. In this kind of problem, a common role of the accountant is to "dollarize" (or to supply the data for "dollarizing") the estimates that are made by technicians.

In the second place, even if it has the knowledge to do so, personnel of the controller's department are in a difficult position when they try to recommend changes in practice to the operating departments. The operating man resents "being told how to do his job" and may reject even workable suggestions. In one factory, eight major changes in operations had been suggested by the accounting department but vetoed by operating men. There is no way of judging whether the accountants or the operators were right, but it was clear that resistance to unasked-for advice was one of the important reasons the suggestions were not considered.

These findings would seem to indicate that, under most circumstances, the controller's department can bring its special skills to bear upon problems most effectively as part of a "team" — formal or informal — which includes staff assistants of operating executives and members of other staff departments. Provided that persons who are responsible to the operating man and in whom he has confidence participate actively in the process, the formal arrangements for participation probably do not matter too much. Observation of "team" participation of this kind, showed wide variation in the extent to which the controller's staff took the initiative or exercised leadership. One factor in this variation was the extent to which accounting considerations were primary or secondary in the problem at hand. Other factors were the professional competence and personality traits of the individuals involved.

Within this framework, development in problem-solving uses of accounting data may be sought in two directions. Perhaps the most important is to assist staff units of operating departments to improve their understanding of the fundamental principles of making cost comparisons. The second is to organize the controller's department so that it is prepared to provide special analyses and reports when these are wanted by the operating departments, and to advise the operating departments on the proper use of accounting data. This does not mean that there is no room for initiative on the part of the controller's department. Quite the contrary, once the basic notion becomes established that the department is a "partner" or co-worker in investigating important problems, there will be ample opportunities for personnel of the controller's department to propose problems that need investigation, to "sell" the usefulness of the help they can provide, and to promote more searching and systematic methods for analyzing operating problems. These goals are most likely to be realized if the controller's department is able to avoid arousing fears of other groups regarding encroachment on their functions and skills.

There are at least three steps involved in this process — although not necessarily in this sequence:

Developing personnel in the controller's department who are themselves thoroughly competent to make economic and operating analyses.

Giving these persons the time, and the responsibility, for keeping closely informed about operating problems.

Developing close contacts with operating men at the strategic decision-making levels.

Care must be taken to develop ample opportunities for the operating departments to use these controller's services, while at the same time leaving with the operating executives the primary initiative for deciding how and when they shall use them. Concrete suggestions as to how such arrangements can be worked out in the factory and the sales department will be offered in the next chapter (pages 74 to 75), and recommendations on the training aspects discussed in Chapter 6, page 98.

ORGANIZING FOR RECORD KEEPING

In organizing for record keeping, the main question is one of geographical location rather than communications: to what extent record-keeping functions should be centrally located; how far they should be decentralized to factories and sales districts.

The analysis of survey data pertaining to organization of record keeping began with identifying records operations according to points of origin of the data. First, there are certain records which originate at decentralized operating locations. Second, there are records functions which can only be performed centrally because they involve consolidation of data into total company records. Further, there are situations where records are kept at intermediate points, that is, data may originate at several operating localities and enter accounting records at some point intermediate to origin and central consolidation.

Observing and analyzing in terms of origin, flow, and use of data, the research team has identified the following factors which influence organization for record keeping in the seven surveyed companies:

Cost considerations.

Accessibility of data for departments other than the controller's department.

Promptness in getting accounting data and reports to users of the information.

Quality of accounting data.

Accounting control.

Special considerations with reference to accounts payable and accounts receivable.

Cost Considerations

In only a few of the observed stituations were accounting costs an important factor in determining the extent of centralization and decentralization. Costs do, of course, impose an outer limit to decentralization. A decentralized operation may be unduly expensive if there is not a sufficient volume of work to permit mechanization of record keeping, where machine methods are applicable, or where there are serious peak loads that could be smoothed out in a larger unit having a greater variety of functions. Once a plant or division scale of operations is reached which permits efficient use of clerical personnel or machine methods, few additional economies of size can be realized through further centralization.

Some data were available in these companies about actual changes that have been made in organization record keeping in recent years. Some of the changes had been in the direction of centralization and some in the direction of decentralization. In only a few cases were costs the major reason for the change. Even in those cases, evidence was scanty that important cost reduction had been realized. In one instance, functions that had been performed at an intermediate (division) level by 56 clerks, were now being performed in the company offices by 44. Further study of the reduction showed that half to two-thirds of it was due to the elimination of divisional profit and loss statements, and only the remainder could be attributed to mechanization or increased utilization of clerical personnel.

The facts developed in this survey lead to the conclusion that costs are a barrier to decentralization only where the decentralized operations produce a very small volume of accounting documents. A very rough rule of thumb might be that decentralized bookkeeping functions in units with fewer than eight or ten clerks are likely to be inefficient from a cost standpoint.

The discussion here has been limited to the actual clerical costs incurred for processing the accounting data. The costs of communications between accounting units, which depend on who needs to have access to particular items of information, have not been considered in reaching this conclusion.

Access to Data

Of considerably greater importance than cost is the need for locating accounting records where the other units which have need for specific pieces of information will have access to them. Here reference is to needs for data beyond those contained in the periodic accounting reports. The most frequently observed needs for access to original records involved:

Data for special studies, *i.e.*, problem-solving data. For example, when labor negotiations are under way, the controller's office may have to refer to the factory accounting departments for certain breakdowns of labor costs.

Data for explanation of variances. For example, a factory department head may want additional detail on his expenditures for supplies.

Questions about customers' orders and accounts receivable. For example, a customer complaint to the sales department might make necessary a reference to the original order, a shipping notice, or an invoice.

Detailed information on costs to quote a price on a special order.

Other questions about the accuracy of classification of the accounting data. For example, a workman may think his pay check incorrect. Or, an

61

accounting clerk in the company offices may find inadequate information for billing on the shipping notice prepared at the factory.

Data on the location and amounts of inventories.

Where problems of this kind were found, the organizational question they raised was one of *geographical location* rather than formal authority. For example, when operating executives in a factory needed supplementary data for a special study, there was no problem of access so long as the factory accounting department had the data. Insofar as the crossing of departmental lines created any problem at all, this was easily solved if adequate accounting services were provided for problem-solving and attention-directing purposes. The same was true when operating executives wanted detailed analyses of particular types of expenditures.

On the other hand, special analysis groups in the company controller's department had a much more difficult task of obtaining data from the factory accounting departments, even though there was no question of crossing departmental lines. So long as data could be obtained in the same factory, there was little or no problem of access; so long as the data were located in the same city, the problems were slight; but where data were located in a different city from the person who needed access to them, the problem was frequently regarded as serious.

Hence the question the controller must ask in fixing the geographical location of record-keeping activities is not: "Who uses the reports?" For most periodic reports, the postal service is an entirely adequate courier. The important question is: "Who, inside and outside the accounting department, has need for access to the detailed records?"

Promptness

A third factor in the location of record-keeping activities is promptness in getting accounting records and reports to their users. Unless very great distances are involved, the time and cost of sending letters and other communications are not critical factors in promptness. Problems of promptness arise primarily from two other causes; first, from delays in handling peak loads, such as month-end closings; second, from the absence of pressure on an accounting unit in one location to take care of requests from another location resulting in a delayed response to such requests.

In none of these problems of promptness does geographical centralization or decentralization appear to be a really important factor. In several interviews, company accounting personnel asserted that centralization would speed up reports because of the need to wait for the factories and sales offices to close their books. On further inquiry, it always turned out that the real difficulty lay in the peak load at closing time, and that this peak would not necessarily be eliminated by centralization.

One specific source of delay in getting out monthly reports is the need to obtain allocations of overhead costs before reports on decentralized factory or sales operations can be completed. This delay arises whether the report is prepared centrally or whether it is prepared at the factory or sales offices. In a previous chapter, it has been argued that decentralization of accounts and decentralized reporting of overhead items can easily be carried too far. The remedy for this delay, in most instances, is to limit decentralized accounts primarily to expenditures which are incurred, and which can be controlled and recorded at the decentralized locations.

One supervisor of a decentralized accounting unit pointed to his ability to mail bills to customers a day earlier, as compared with the former centralized billing arrangement. Most executives in controllers' departments, however, were not impressed with one day more or less in billing. Similarly, there were some comments that if accounts payable are handled at the factory, it is easier to pay in time to take discounts. Yet, other companies have found it possible to pay bills promptly and take discounts without decentralizing.

In many cases where promptness was a problem, the time requirements were met without changing geographical location of the bookkeeping functions. The telephone or teletype was sometimes used to send in preliminary data or data needed for closings. Maintaining copies of certain records sometimes solved the problems of promptness and accessibility. Survey observations indicate that careful procedures work can solve most problems of promptness without geographical relocation of record-keeping functions unless direct access to records is involved as well. A good example of this approach, in a company where credit activities and accounts receivable were completely centralized geographically, is the following:

"Don't the sales people say you're taking too long in approving credit risks?"

"The salesman gives us the names of two or three possible dealers in a town. We check their credit ratings before he calls on them. We have teletype and phone contacts with sales branches for matters that require immediate action."

We are not suggesting that this particular solution fits all companies, but rather that the promptness problem should not be overestimated in determining the geographical location of record-keeping functions.

Quality of Accounting Information

There are really two problems of quality. One of them tends to be recognized by the accounting personnel responsible for the company financial statements; the other by the accounting personnel at decentralized locations.

The first problem — that of uniformity — is to make certain that data are classified in the same way at all the factories and all the sales offices. This requirement was frequently used as an argument against further decentralization. Yet in those companies where decentralization has been carried furthest, uniformity is not regarded as a serious problem — at least it is considered a solvable one. The steps that have been taken to solve it are to prepare cards of accounts, to issue relatively detailed accounting procedures, to supervise their installation in the decentralized accounting locations, and to rely upon internal auditors (and public auditors) to detect nonstandard practices. Uniformity appears to have been achieved in the companies that have had time to "shake down" their accounting procedures. It is of somewhat greater concern in companies that have been recently engaged in extensive changes in their accounting systems.

The second problem of quality — and, possibly, the more important one — is to see that accounting data accurately describe and reflect transactions and operations actually taking place. No amount of attention to uniformity can assure this if the original source data or the systems for handling the data are poor. The only place where the source data can be improved is at the point where they originate — by comparing the data with the facts. Only to a very limited extent can mistakes in classification or recording made at this initial stage be corrected by checking or comparing pieces of paper.

Where accounting personnel have had experience with both geographically centralized and decentralized record-keeping organizations, they were emphatic as to the improvement accomplished by decentralization of original records. Here are some typical comments:

"No entries should be made unless they are understood, and it would be very hard to understand things from this distance (the company office). It is much better to have them made where the basic information is developed."

"We had problems of uniformity at first, but we are over that hump. We have a uniform set of accounts and the definitions are pretty strictly adhered to. The only place we can get out of line is where they make out the customer's account and don't put in the proper item."

"Decentralization is better because it puts the record keepers closer to the work. They know what the product is. If something is wrong with the shipping notice, they can go to the shipping department and correct it."

"The accounting people are so far removed that they don't know the value of the product. They may change the decimal point — $500 for $50. If they were here and knew what the product looks like, they wouldn't make those mistakes."

Accounting Control

Most of the surveyed companies have an internal auditing division in the controller's department, and use traveling auditors to check the decentralized operations and establish and maintain uniformity. This control, supplemented by independent audits, was regarded as adequate. No objections were raised to geographical decentralization on the basis of the need for better control. One qualification, however, with reference to accounts payable, will be discussed below.

One company has developed a system of resident auditors which seems to operate as effectively as the traveling audit used by the others. Certain safeguards are taken to protect the independence of the auditors:

"These men are on the ground at all times. They learn intimate details of local organization — not too intimate, I hope. I can honestly say that in all my visits, I have failed to find a single instance of lack of independence on the part of the auditors. We don't locate a man on a permanent basis, but move him from time to time. In addition, we frequently borrow a man from one location to assist in another. There are real morale advantages in having resident auditors. Most men don't like constant traveling on the job and it can easily get them into trouble."

These comments of a company accounting executive were confirmed by observations of the resident auditors at the decentralized locations.

Recapitulation: Decentralization of Record Keeping

The most important criteria to be considered in the geographical decentralization of records functions are the accessibility of documents and the reliability of the source records. Both of these criteria point in the direction of relatively great decentralization.

There may be definite cost advantages in centralization to whatever extent is required to gain the advantages of clerical specialization and mechanization. Once a sufficient volume of transactions is attained for this purpose, however, further centralization brings only a slight return in economy.

Questions of promptness, over-all uniformity in classification and auditing control are of small importance in determining the optimal degree of geographical centralization or decentralization.

Further discussion of factory accounting and decentralized sales accounting will be found in the next chapter. Before concluding this section, however, a few more comments are necessary on some accounting problems which involve more than one department. These comments present the composite experience of the companies surveyed.

Accounts payable. There are several possible locations for accounts payable work, particularly if the purchasing function is centralized while the commodities purchased are received by decentralized factories. Where purchasing and receiving are geographically separated, quantities can be omitted from that copy of the voucher which is transmitted to the receiving clerk to insure a careful check of the shipment. Receipt of the shipment can then be acknowledged to the accounts payable section in the company accounting office and payment made there. This has an additional advantage where several factories are receiving goods from the same vendor.

The chief problem that has to be solved if accounts payable are centralized is to avoid delays in charging purchases to factory cost accounts. Factory department heads are inconvenienced if they cannot predict when items which they have purchased are going to be charged against their accounts, and if the charges are not recorded promptly. There are various devices that will assist in keeping charges current even when accounting for payables is centralized. In many situations it is possible to make the initial charges from receiving reports, without waiting for an invoice or for the posting of the purchase to accounts payable.

Accounts receivable. Sales involve even more complicated interdepartmental relations than do purchases. The sales department, the credit division (in sales, accounting, or treasury departments), the factory (production scheduling, manufacturing, and shipping departments), and the billing and accounts receivable units in the accounting department, are all concerned at one stage or another in the process. One variable is the location of the credit function, a second, the location where invoices are prepared, and a third, the location where accounts receivable are posted.

Considerations other than bookkeeping convenience will often determine whether the credit function is to be centralized or decentralized. Where customers are small local retail concerns, there may be advantages in decentralizing credit management although an example of an effective system of centralized credit determination under these circumstances has already been mentioned. Where customers are large concerns, themselves geographically decentralized, the balance of advantages will generally be on the side of a relatively centralized credit function.

Survey evidence indicates that, primarily for reasons of access to records, there are noticeable advantages in locating accounts receivable in the same city or cities

65

as the credit management units. But for clerical economy in posting this implies that credit work should not be further decentralized than is thought to be absolutely necessary.

In none of the companies was the problem of locating billing a particularly critical one. There was a tendency to organize it in one way for sales made from company operated branches, another way for sales made from factories. In the former case, locating the billing function with accounts receivable and collections generally appears to be the most satisfactory solution. In the latter case, the advantages seem fairly balanced between billing at the factory, or alternatively, sending a copy of the shipping memorandum to a central billing unit located with accounts receivable.[3] Provided there is a sufficient volume of transactions for clerical economy, either arrangement appears to work satisfactorily.

INTERNAL ORGANIZATION OF ACCOUNTING FUNCTIONS

Earlier in this chapter, general conclusions were presented about organizing the controller's department so as to encourage and assist in the use of accounting data for attention-directing and problem-solving purposes. Findings about geographical decentralization of actual record keeping have also been discussed with reference to such uses of accounting data.

These conclusions also lead to an examination of how various analytical services are to be set up in the organizational structure of controllers' departments, and how they are to be related to record keeping and report preparation.

The evidence indicates that a considerable degree of separation is desirable between the record-keeping and regular reporting functions, and the analytical or "service" function in the controller's department. It does not appear to be effective to give the same unit major responsibilities for record keeping and for special service functions involving frequent direct contact with the operating executives. To a lesser extent, it seems desirable to develop some specialization between personnel responsible for variance explanations, standards changes, or other services connected with attention-directing functions, and personnel responsible for special studies falling into the problem-solving category.

Perhaps the principal need for separating these functions is to maintain adequate administrative direction and control over the amount of time and effort that is devoted by accounting personnel to different kinds of tasks. It was repeatedly found that special reporting and analytical services to operating executives were crowded out in favor of "bookkeeping" activities where one supervisor was responsible for both functions. To a noticeable extent, responsibilities for explaining variances and for revising standards tended to crowd out responsibilities for making special studies. The main reason is obvious — deadlines for periodic accounting reports are frequent, definite and imperative. Analytical work tends to get done in the intervals (if any) between report deadlines. Failure to meet deadlines on periodic reports results in immediate and strong repercussions from superiors in the controller's department; neglecting analytical work leads to much milder reactions.

---

[3] There are some companies, not among those included in this study, where customers insist that invoices accompany shipment. This would almost require, of course, that invoices be prepared at the factory.

Thus, survey findings show that when these functions are combined in one unit, the controller's department retains little control over the amount of effort to be given to each.

Such combination leads to a potential conflict between the controller's responsibility of assisting operating executives and his function of analyst and consultant to other executives of the company. This is not to say that the operating man consciously and deliberately puts pressure on the accountant to falsify his data, or to present an inaccurately favorable picture of what is going on. However, operating men do frequently request reclassifications of charges and revisions of standards, and there is a feeling that an accountant who is wholly on the operating man's "team" is in a poor position to handle such matters. In some cases even the operating executives share this feeling — as suggested by the following excerpt from an interview with a department head:

"Would you rather have a cost man attached to the accounting department or a man of your own down here?"

"An accounting man. To be of the greatest use, he would have to head up the place where the data are available and then, too, he shouldn't be a special pleader for me. He should be neutral."

The tradition is strong in the accounting profession that the accountant, like Caesar's wife, must be above suspicion. Persons interviewed often mention this insistence on independence as a basis for limiting the closeness of relationship between the controller's department and operating departments. A rather extreme example of this attitude is the following comment of a member of a controller's staff:

"What would be the effect if you placed the factory accounting executives under factory managers?"

"Well, that would mean that we would weaken our control over them. Nothing would ever be said to the controller if the factory manager was concerned about something else. Another thing is that we would have difficulty in making sure that expense items were handled properly. It is very important that we have a free hand in being able to tell company management what is going on. We do need a sense of independence in the accounting department at the factory. We don't trust anybody. You know that the biggest shortages are always caused by trusted employees. One of our interests in the accounting department is to keep people honest."

This study did not provide any evidence that maintaining the independence of the accountant is, in fact, a serious problem. But results do suggest that separating accounting from other controllership functions (assuming an effective internal audit unit at company level) helps remove dangers of collusion. It also helps to give the controller's personnel who are charged with providing service to the operating departments greater freedom to develop close working relationships without a feeling of conflicting responsibilities.

A third reason for separating these important functions of the controller's department is to give a greater flexibility in organizing each of the separate functions in the most economical and effective manner. It should be clear by now that the amount of centralization or decentralization that is optimal for the record-keeping functions is not necessarily the same as for other functions. It has been further pointed out, that the levels at which units can provide effective attention-directing service are different from the levels at which assistance can best be provided in problem solving. If there is some organizational separation of these functions, each can be located at the level or levels most appropriate for its particular task.

In the next chapter, a scheme is proposed which is suitable to large factories. It provides —

Budget and variance analysis assistance primarily at the departmental level.

Assistance in special studies at the factory level in close cooperation with other staff departments.

Record keeping through relatively centralized factory-level units.

In the case of analytical and service functions, the primary criterion to guide organization is the need for horizontal channels of communication. In the case of record-keeping functions, the most important criteria are cost, access to information, promptness in preparing reports, uniformity in records procedures, and control from an auditing standpoint.

If the record-keeping functions of the controller's department are separated from the others in this manner, two problems of communication must be solved.

The first problem is that of transmission of periodic reports and other accounting data to units which provide analytical and other special services to operating departments. This is a relatively simple problem. The information that is transmitted is systematic, objective, and routine. Within the controller's department, responsibility for its interpretation and its application to operating problems rests primarily with its users — that is, the analytical personnel — rather than with the units which record the data and prepare these reports. The difficult problem is not how to get accounting information from the accounting records and reports into the hands of accountants, but how to bridge the next gap in the communications chain and bring these data to bear upon the operating problems. For this reason, the survey team concludes that it is of no great importance that the record-keeping and service functions be performed by the same units in the controller's department simply for the purpose of keeping these in closer contact. Survey interviews and observed facts do not indicate that this is really a serious problem or that, if it is a problem at all, it requires this particular organizational solution. It is far more important to have a separate analytical and consultative unit free to make frequent, direct contacts with operating personnel.

The second of these problems relates to communicating instructions on procedures and standards revisions to various accounting units. No special difficulties were observed when the accounting unit responsible for determining procedures, or the unit responsible for standards revision, were separate from the units that performed the record-keeping functions. The instructions that need to be given to the record-keeping units can be set out in writing. They do not require continuous direct supervision to be effected. This is not to say that the units can operate in isolation, but that, with good working relations between their supervisors, the tasks can be handled effectively and without creating internal confusion or too complex a pattern of relationships.

68

ORGANIZATION STRUCTURE OF THE CONTROLLER'S DEPARTMENT

The final task in this chapter is to put together the various pieces of the controller's department which have been discussed in previous sections. What are the main units into which the department should be divided for purposes of supervision?

The main alternatives for organizing top-level controllership are the so-called "divisional" and "functional" arrangements, respectively. Under a divisional plan, the principal subordinates of the company controller are divisional controllers, each responsible for a complete system of sales, manufacturing, and general accounting for some one division of the company's operations. Under a functional plan, the principal subordinates of the company controller are executives responsible for particular activities like general accounting, sales accounting, budgeting, cost planning, analysis, and so on.

Clearly, a divisional plan is appropriate only if the company is operated on a divisional basis and only if the divisions are sufficiently independent so that it is thought desirable to provide detailed accounting reports and information for the respective divisions. Whether this form of organization is to be adopted depends on the prior decision, discussed in the last chapter, as to whether the accounts and reports are to be decentralized. Without divisional decentralization of accounts there appear to be no substantial advantages in operating with divisional controllers.[4]

If it is proposed to organize in terms of controllership functions, a decision must still be reached as to which way the cake is to be cut. There are at least two main possibilities:

A classification of functions that parallels, as far as possible, the operating departments.
A classification of functions like that followed in this chapter, which separates record keeping, attention-directing services, and problem-solving services.

Main functions under the first alternative are:

General accounting.
Manufacturing accounting.
Sales accounting.
Accounting for other departments.

The main functions under the second alternative are:

Financial accounting.
Cost accounting and report preparation.
Cost planning and analysis.
Special accounting studies.
Internal audit.

---

[4] This does not imply, of course, that the company controller should not approve the chart of accounts, but refers to the breakdown of accounting information to parallel the organization structure.

There are any number of possible cross-classifications of these two basic schemes and a corresponding number of plans for organization of the controller's department.

Without insisting on its unique virtues, a plan that would be consistent with the conclusions reached about centralization and decentralization and about the separation of functions would be the following:

A. General accounting (record keeping and periodic reports)
   1. Financial statements
   2. Consolidation of manufacturing accounts
   3. Supervision of decentralized factory accounting (see Chapter 5, pages 80 to 81)
   4. Accounts payable (if centralized)
   5. Tax accounting
B. Sales accounting (records, periodic reports, and current analysis)
   1. Accounts receivable (if centralized)
   2. Credits and collections (if in controller's department)
   3. Supervision and data consolidation for decentralized sales accounting
   4. Current analysis of periodic accounting reports for company-level sales executives
C. Cost planning and analysis
   1. Development and installation of manufacturing cost accounting procedures
   2. Company-level review of cost standards
   3. Current analysis of manufacturing costs for company-level production executives
D. Special studies
   1. Studies of capital appropriations, investment policy, marketing problems, and other company-level problems where accounting data are relevant and periodic reports not suitable.
   2. Development in cooperation with other departments of improved procedures for economic analysis of company problems
   3. Assistance to decentralized special studies units
E. Internal audit (usual functions)

Figure 2 illustrates this plan which represents a combination of the two bases of functional classification mentioned above. Below the organization chart are shown the main responsibilities of each of the five divisions of the controller's department.

The organization plan described here is not particularly revolutionary, and indeed, is similar to the structure observed in several of the company controllers' departments included in the study. The usual questions can be raised about the jurisdictional boundaries between the five major units. However, the boundaries appear to be capable of as clear definition under this plan as under the other possible arrangements.

Once the division of work among the major company-level divisions in the controller's department has been fixed, there remains the question of their relations with the geographically decentralized units located at factories and regional or district sales offices. This question will be explored in the next chapter.

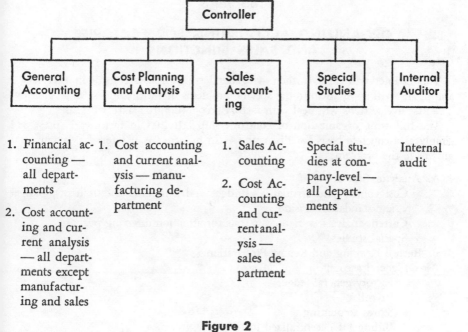

Figure 2

PROPOSED COMPANY-WIDE CONTROLLER'S ORGANIZATION

71

Chapter 5

ORGANIZING ACCOUNTING FOR FACTORIES
AND SALES FUNCTIONS

This chapter will carry further the general conclusions set forth in Chapters 3 and 4, and will apply them to the specific problems of factory and sales accounting. The first five sections will deal with factory accounting, the sixth with sales.

The following organization of controllership activities in factories is presented simply as a concrete basis for discussion — in no sense is it offered as a universal answer to the problem:

A. Analytic Services
   Cost control and standards: Budget and standards determinants, budget and standards revision
   Current analysis: variance analysis for attention-directing purposes
   Special studies
B. Record Keeping and Report Preparation
   General accounting
   Factory general ledger
   Payroll
   Stores accounting
   Billing (if decentralized to factory)
   Machine tabulation
   Cost accounting ledgers and reports
   Time and production recording
   Accounting procedures

This classification reflects survey findings discussed in the preceding chapter, particularly the conclusion expressed there with reference to the company office, namely, that there is a net advantage in separating analytical and service from record-keeping activities of the controller's department. One of the tasks in this chapter is to assess the workability of such separation at the factory office. Under this scheme the two principal subordinates of the factory chief accountant would be an assistant in charge of record keeping and periodic reports, another in charge of the analytical services. The organization of the analytical and service functions will be discussed first, then the organization of the record-keeping functions, then the relation between them, and finally the organizational relationships between the factory accounting department and the company offices.

FACTORIES: ANALYTICAL AND SERVICE FUNCTIONS

Except in a very large factory, the analytical functions will involve a relatively small number of full-time employees. This is one reason for suggesting that the analytical services should be grouped together — such a grouping permits greater flexibility in the use of staff. Another reason is that the various analytical functions are interrelated. It is important that there be close working relationships and communication among the persons doing the analytical and service work.

Cost Control and Standards

Based on survey observations and data, the conclusion has been reached that establishment of budgets and cost standards is a joint responsibility shared with the operating departments. The first responsibility of the controller's department in this area is one of translating operating data and the standards into dollars and subsequently reporting back the comparison of actual performance with the standard.

Since the operating executives will be accustomed to working with the analytical personnel and will rely on the latter as their primary channel of communication with the controller's department at headquarters, cooperation in setting and revising of budgets and standards can best be handled through these same channels.

Observation in all the surveyed factories show that maintenance of the budget and standards requires contact with operating personnel at all key stages of factory and company organization. The manufacturing and industrial engineering department contacts are extremely important for learning about dissatisfaction with standards for whatever reason, and for learning about changes in operating practices which require standards revisions. The importance of the contact with the factory manager and the industrial engineering department is obvious.

Since cost, budget and standards decisions may require changes in record-keeping activities, it might be argued that they should be associated with the record-keeping unit rather than the analytical unit. Some evidence bearing on this point was obtained in the factories that had both analytical personnel and a separate unit for gathering time and production data. While operating personnel in these factories had contacts with both analysts, and time and production personnel, they tended to use the latter channels primarily for raising questions about individual paychecks — for example, incorrect incentive calculations — and resorted to the analysts when the standards themselves were in question. One reason for this is that the operating people did not find it effective to go through several levels of clerical personnel on questions of standards. Another reason is that questions of standards frequently arose as a result of the analysis of variances, when the cost analyst was already in the picture. This type of evidence is the basis for the conclusion that separation of the cost budgeting from the record-keeping function at the factory does not interfere with standards revision, so far as operating departments are concerned.

A further point must be examined, however. Does not this separation involve an unnecessary number of people in carrying out standards changes and does it not create actual or potential conflicts of authority for those maintaining cost records? The survey team found no evidence of excess personnel requirements or of conflict. As long as there is a close working relationship between the supervisor of the cost control and standards work and the supervisor of the unit responsible for cost records in the factory, there is little apparent difficulty in carry-

73

ing out standards changes. Factory accounting departments are small enough to make it easy to establish such a relationship, and it appeared to be satisfactory in the situations studied.

Attention Directing: Current Analysis

The key to effective current analysis is good horizontal communication with the factory department heads. Survey data indicate that in a large factory (one thousand employees and over) there may be a sufficient volume of current analytical work to justify assignment of a cost analyst to each operating department or group of departments. Where physical arrangements make this possible, it is advantageous to give the analyst a desk located in the factory, close to the department head, and another located in the factory cost control and analysis unit. The analyst, moreover, should be encouraged to divide his time between these two locations. Two examples may be cited of procedures which were observed to be effective for current analysis.

In one factory, a junior supervisory employee in the accounting department contacts each operating department head as soon as the daily reports of direct costs are ready. He obtains from the department head an explanation of variances that are larger than a specified limit. These explanations are entered on the cost reports. The annotated cost reports are then transmitted to the factory manager, the production manager, and the department head. In this particular factory, the accounting man does not question or edit the operating man's explanations. The production manager reviews the reports closely and department heads expect to hear from him promptly for further discussion of large or unusual variances.

In a second factory, junior accounting employees prepare monthly explanations of variances for the operating departments to which they are assigned. Generally, they talk to the department heads in the course of preparing the explanations, and in about half the departments they go over the report with the department head before presenting it to the top cost analyst in the factory accounting department. The department heads do not, however, formally approve the explanations and do not in all cases agree with the reasons given for variances.

The former procedure is well suited to smaller factories where the variance analysis work can be handled by one or two analysts located in the accounting offices. Its success depends heavily on the factory manager's or production manager's continuing attention to the reports. When the department heads know that the factory manager wants the data, and when the accounting man accepts the explanations they give, the fact that the requests are made by someone in another department in a relatively low-status position does not cause resentment. The first procedure does not encourage development of as close working relationship between the junior accountant and the operating executives as does the second procedure.

In the factories using the second procedure, support was again received from factory managers who hold monthly cost meetings at which the reports are discussed. In a few instances where the operating man definitely disagreed with an explanation provided by the accounting department, vigorous protest was made to accounting. As a result, the accounting personnel are quite careful to check any explanations about which they are in doubt. In many cases they rely heavily on the operating men for the explanations. Nevertheless, the accounting personnel feel that when they have a real disagreement as to the reason for a variance, they have a responsibility to include in their reports both their own explanation and that of the operating man.

If the actual variance analysis work is done by assistants who are outside the factory accounting department and attached directly to the operating executives, a single individual of fairly senior status may be able to handle the accounting department's part of the current analysis work. His primary task would be to maintain liaison with the analysts in the operating departments, aiding them to obtain data from the accounting records. Such factory organization and procedure was not observed in this study, but there appears to be no reason why such an arrangement would not work well. This assumes clearly established responsibility in the operating departments to make thorough and systematic analyses of their costs.

Problem-Solving Analyses: Special Studies

Special studies work at the factory originates primarily from two sources:

Requests from the factory manager and factory staff departments like industrial engineering.

Requests from special analysis units at the company office for additional data needed for their work.

In addition, an alert and effectively staffed accounting unit may itself initiate special analyses. A large majority of the special studies that were made by the surveyed factory accounting and control departments involved problems relating to more than one factory department. For these reasons, a single special-studies unit in the factory would be more effective than a number of decentralized departmental units.[1] This is borne out by the fact that, even in the factory which had gone furthest in the creation of decentralized departmental accounting units, most of the special studies work was not being done in such units but in the central cost control and analysis unit.

Considerations of clerical economy also point toward centralization of the special studies unit. Since the volume of special analysis work for any one factory department fluctuates greatly, the necessary clerical and statistical services are more economically provided by a single unit. Finally, it has been noted that personnel who have sufficient understanding of the economic significance of accounting data to plan and carry out good cost analyses are extremely rare. So long as this kind of human resource is scarce, centralization will make for most effective utilization of these skills and abilities.

Relations Among the Analytical Services

What is suggested, then, is that a senior accounting executive in the factory supervise the special analytical services, and that the work under his direction be further delegated to three units:

---

[1] This may not hold, of course, in an extremely large factory composed of several relatively self-contained departments making different products. At a factory like Kodak Park Works of Eastman Kodak, for example, the factory division may be the appropriate level for much of the special studies work.

A centralized factory cost planning unit.
A decentralized current analysis unit, and
A centralized factory special studies unit.

In a small factory, each of these "units" may be virtually a one-man operation, and it would be unwise to insist on too sharp a division of functions. In a large factory, each might consist of a staff of a half dozen or more accountants and analysts, together with clerical assistance. The size of the units, particularly of the current analysis unit, will be determined not only by the size of the factory, but also by the extent to which the operating departments themselves assume responsibility for analysis.

In speaking of separate units, the survey team has in mind direct supervision (that is, formal authority) and work assignments. The small size of staff required for the service functions, if these are separate from the record-keeping functions, should provide some safeguard against excessive subdivision and isolation. The current analysis unit, in particular, is an important source of information to the cost planning unit on situations that need to be investigated for possible changes in standards, and to the special studies unit on possible problems for study.

The cost planning and statistics bureau at the National Works of National Tube is an example of an arrangement along the lines suggested here. The supervisor of the bureau has two assistants — one for cost control and standards and one for analysis and special studies. These two assistants direct the work of senior and junior cost analysts. There is considerable flexibility in the assignment of the analysts. They may spend several months working on a standards revision under the assistant for cost control, then be assigned to current analysis in an operating department, and at still another time to make a special study. These shifts in personnel are a major factor in preventing isolation of the current analysis staff from the staff engaged in planning and special studies. Such shifts also provide the analysts with well-rounded and progressively responsible experience in all aspects of analytical work.

Two weaknesses were apparent in the operation of the unit. First, placing both current analysis and special studies under the direction of the same assistant led to insufficient emphasis on special studies. Second, probably too much rather than too little use was made of the flexibility built into the arrangement. When analysts are too frequently withdrawn from their departmental assignments, it is difficult to develop close relationships with the operating department heads. Since the same effect of frequent rotation of assignments was noticed in one or two other factories, it suggests that accounting personnel assigned to current analysis work should probably not be reassigned more frequently than once a year. There may be no serious objection to *brief* special assignments that do not interrupt for more than a few days the contact with the operating department.

FACTORIES: RECORD-KEEPING FUNCTIONS

The chief issue, in factory accounting, with respect to the record-keeping functions, is whether they should be subdivided into units corresponding to the major accounting activities, as suggested in the outline at the beginning of this chapter, or whether they should be subdivided and decentralized into units paralleling the several operating departments. The former plan may be regarded as centralized at the factory level, the latter as functionally decentralized to the operating department level. On the basis of this study, the survey team concluded that the net advantage lies on the side of the centralized organization structure described above. This conclusion might have to be modified in a very large factory (say, having 5,000 or more employees) spread out over a considerable area. The evidence for this finding is discussed in the following section.

Cost

In the absence of means for direct cost comparisons, the interviewers asked what differences it would make, from a clerical standpoint, whether record-keeping activities were centralized or decentralized. Replies obtained and direct observation indicate the most important point of difference was that a geographically centralized set-up would be required, at least to the extent that mechanical tabulating was to be substituted for manual methods. Hence, the centralized arrangement is to be preferred for those operations of recording and report preparation where machine methods can be more economical than manual methods.

With respect to manual accounting procedures, gains in efficiency from centralization are not likely to be great, except in the very small factory where the decentralized arrangement is hardly feasible. One reason for this is that, in large- and medium-size factories, the actual division of work among *individual* clerks is often very much the same regardless of centralization or decentralization of the organizational units. For example, the payroll unit in the centralized organization of one factory was found to be divided into sections, each performing the payroll work for a different group of operating departments. Similar schemes of subdivision were found in the time and production recording unit, and the cost accounting unit of the same factory. Schematically, the organization plan was this:

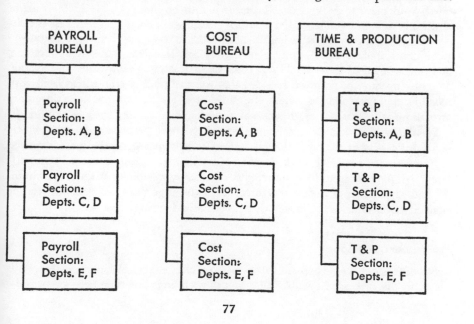

The difference between the centralized and decentralized set-up is primarily one of formal authority and supervision. By simply regrouping the nine sections, and without changing the work assignment of a single clerk, this "centralized" supervisory arrangement could be changed to a "decentralized" arrangement:

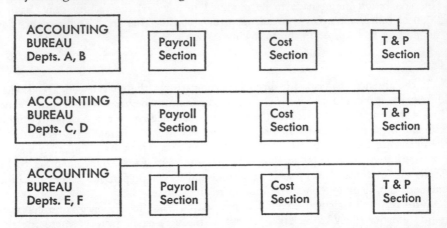

It is hard to see how the rearrangement of the boxes representing the individual sections could be expected to affect clerical costs very much, one way or the other. Under both plans there is some specialization in performance of each major accounting function for each major group of operating units. The only real difference is in the way in which these ultimate specializations are combined for supervisory purposes, and this does not seem to have an important bearing on clerical economy.

It is conceivable that one of these arrangements or the other would be more effective in meeting peak clerical loads or would be more flexible in the case of absence of one or two clerks. On *a priori* grounds, one would suspect that the decentralized arrangement could absorb peak loads more easily because each bureau would be responsible for a variety of accounting functions rather than just one, and peaks of all of these would not come at precisely the same time. Observation of actual operations, however, revealed that the main peaks (those associated with monthly closings) occur at almost the same time for payroll, cost, and inventory accounting, and that not much smoothing of loads is accomplished by grouping.

Flexibility in case a clerk is ill or absent need be a problem only in extremely small units — units too small for clerical economy. In larger units there appeared to be no reason why each clerk should not be trained to handle two or three different assignments in order to provide the necessary flexibility. With proper training and supervision of the clerical force, about the same degree of flexibility can be attained under either a centralized or a decentralized arrangement.

Promptness of Reports

No differences were observed to result from clerical centralization or decentralization in the promptness with which monthly closings are completed or periodic reports issued. Where an attempt is made to prepare monthly reports in the decentralized units, some back-tracking is necessary in the sense of data going from the decentralized units to the tabulating units and back again. But this should cause no significant delay if other steps are completed on schedule.

Access to Data

In a large factory, operating department executives may have better access to records with a decentralized arrangement — particularly with decentralized supervision and actual physical decentralization, with the clerks located in the factory departments. On the other hand, where adequate current analysis service was provided, analysts were able to obtain needed information from the central records unit without noticeable difficulty. Moreover, in the decentralized arrangement, information requested by department heads was often found to be dispersed among several locations as, for example, stores record unit or the maintenance and repair department. Hence, from the standpoint of access, decentralization of clerical activities is of no great value.

Quality

Under any arrangement, time and production data come initially from the operating locations. If the controller's department has the responsibility for recording this information, clerks must be located in the factory. The important question here is which plan of organization will provide the best supervision of the time and production clerks. In a factory operating on three shifts, it may be more economical — require fewer supervisors — to provide this supervision from a single time and production bureau, since the payroll and cost units will generally operate on a single-shift basis. In a factory operating on a single shift, it was not observed that there are decisive advantages one way or the other. If the basic time and production data are recorded by operating personnel or by a separate inspection department, there is even less basis for choosing between the two arrangements.

Supervision

From the standpoint of the factory controller or accounting executive, the centralized arrangement appears to have several advantages. Changes in procedures and standards, particularly those originating in the company headquarters offices, frequently affect payroll procedures in *all* departments or cost procedures in *all* departments. Effecting these changes in the factory accounting department is simpler if there is one supervisor for all payroll activities, one for cost records, and one for time and production records. In the decentralized arrangement, all the supervisors of the clerical divisions must be involved in each such change. There was some evidence that procedural changes were more complicated, from an administrative standpoint, in those factories which had decentralized their clerical activities.

Conclusions drawn from survey data in the preceding chapter indicated strong advantages in decentralizing factory accounting to the factory office at least. Facts

79

considered in this chapter indicate, though less decisively, that there are also net advantages to centralizing factory record keeping in the factory office rather than decentralizing it to various factory operating departments. The larger the factory and the greater the independence of departments within the factory, the less decisive the advantages of such centralization. But even in factories with around 5,000 employees, no evidence was found that a decentralized arrangement was advantageous.

ORGANIZATION OF FACTORY ACCOUNTING SUPERVISION

One aspect of centralization and decentralization of factory accounting has been largely omitted from the preceding discussion since it relates both to analytical services and to record keeping. The decision to centralize or decentralize within the factory leads to differences in the form of supervision for the organization.

Under a decentralized plan,[2] a somewhat different supervisory structure is required. The work falls into three units:

Analytical services — somewhat narrower in scope than under the other plan since some of the services are assigned to the decentralized units.

General accounting — all record-keeping functions that are not decentralized.

Decentralized departmental accounting. To provide adequate supervision to the decentralized units, the heads of these generally report to a supervisor of departmental accounting units.

With this decentralized plan, all three principal subordinates of the factory accountant (the heads of analytical services, general accounting, and departmental accounting units) of necessity have major contact with the individual departmental units. Nominally, the individual departmental accounting supervisors report to one man. However, it was our observation that if the system is to operate smoothly and effectively these supervisors must accept a great deal of administrative direction (usually referred to as "functional supervision") from the other two top-level supervisors. The general accounting supervisor depends upon them for the basic data on which the general accounting reports are based, and is primarily responsible for enforcing their observance of the company-wide accounting standards and practices. On the other hand, the supervisor of analytical services depends on the departmental units to carry out policies on standard costs, and to execute analysis assignments.

In a factory where this arrangement prevailed, we found that the individual departmental accounting units had need of more frequent communication with the supervisors of general accounting and of analytical services than they did with their nominal superior — the supervisor of departmental accounting units. This was reinforced by the fact that requests for information, directives, and communications from the company offices to the factory tended to follow functional channels, and hence often to by-pass the supervisor of the departmental accounting units.[3]

[2] The supervisory structure under the centralized plan was discussed on pp. 79-80.

[3] The relations between the company's and the factory controller's departments will be discussed more fully on pp. 81 ff.

In this factory, the decentralized arrangement worked quite smoothly. It was apparent, however, that it worked largely because the participants were not strict in their observance of formal channels, and because the head of the departmental accounting units tended, in fact, to operate as assistant factory accountant rather than as head of the decentralized units. Hence, the best that can be said for the formal authority relationships in this factory is that they did not interfere too seriously with the effective informal operation of the organization. A supervisor of the departmental units who did not allow informal by-passing would probably soon reveal the weaknesses of the formal organizational arrangement.

Again, it is important not to exaggerate the differences between the two organizational plans. The individual accounting units in the centralized set-up are by no means completely self-contained or unrelated to each other. In particular, putting into effect standards changes requires the same kind of cooperation between the cost accounting unit and the cost control and standards unit of a centralized set-up as is required between departmental accounting units and cost control in the decentralized set-up. Nevertheless, on balance, survey observations indicate that the flow of internal organization communications on matters of work assignments and policy changes was somewhat smoother and simpler in the centralized than in the decentralized factory accounting organization.

RELATIONS BETWEEN FACTORY AND HOME OFFICE

In a controller's department organized along the lines outlined here — with decentralized factory accounting — the factory accountant [4] is a key man. He provides the main link in the chain of authority between the company and the factory accounting personnel. Generally he is the company's top accounting representative in the city where he is located. He is the key link in the important horizontal communications chain between the company controller's department and other factory executives. For these reasons he is a central figure in any discussion of the relations between the company controller's department and the factory accounting and control department.

The Factory Accountant

It may be well to review briefly the description in Chapter 2 of the authority relations of the factory accountant with the company controller and the factory manager, respectively. In three companies the authority is centralized — the factory accountant is both administratively and functionally responsible to the accounting department. In four companies both the company controller and the factory manager have some degree of formal authority over the factory accountant.

A comparison of these two groups of companies gives a basis for evaluating the importance of "unity of command" in this particular situation, hence the relative advantages of centralized as against decentralized formal authority over the factory accountant. Are any difficulties created when the factory accountant has two

---

[4] To avoid confusion with various titles used to describe similar responsibilities for the company as a whole, the term "factory accountant" is used to designate the chief accounting and control executive of a factory.

bosses? Are there any compensating advantages to the arrangement? Let us see, first of all, what was learned from interviews and observations at the factories.

In three factories where the factory manager had no formal authority over the factory accountant, the loyalties of the latter were pretty clearly with the controller's department rather than the factory. In five of six factories where the authority over the factory accountant was divided, his loyalty to the factory manager appeared to be somewhat stronger than his loyalty to the accounting department.

In two of the six factories where authority was divided, the factory accountant felt himself to be in a "cross-pressure" situation, where conflicting demands were being made upon his loyalty. In one of these two factories, the factory accountant felt considerable loyalty to the factory manager and some antagonism toward the company controller's department; in the other, there was considerable antagonism between the factory manager and the factory accountant. These two factories, incidentally, were in different companies. In the other four factories where authority was divided, there was no indication that the accountant felt himself subject to cross-pressures.

The two groups of factories cannot be distinguished on the basis of the amount of accounting service provided to factory management. Two of the three factories where authority was centralized ranked very high in this respect, and there were close working relations between the factory accounting department and the operating management. But the same can be said of the four factories with divided authority where there was not serious cross-pressure, and of one of the two in which cross-pressure situations existed.

In all nine factories, regardless of formal authority, the factory accountant turned to the company controller for his instructions and approval on accounting and control procedure.

Except in one of the two cross-pressure situations, the fact that a factory accountant identified himself with the controller's department did not cause him to be less concerned than the other factory accountants with the service he was providing to factory management. The absence of formal authority did not prevent the factory manager from exercising about as much inflence over the work of the accounting department — the kinds of reports received, and the initiation of special studies — as in factories where he had such authority.

Omitting the two factories where a cross-pressure situation existed, there is very little distinction that can be traced to formal authority between the three factories in which authority is centralized in the controller's department and the four in which authority over the factory accountant is exercised jointly by the controller's department and the factory manager. There was some difference in the balance of loyalties of the accounting personnel, but no observable difference in the effectiveness of accounting service to the factory management. The *actual* exercise of authority — as distinguished from the designation of *formal* authority — of company controller or his assistant and of factory manager, respectively, over the factory accountant was very similar in all seven factories. From the evidence of these seven factories, it is concluded that unity of command is rather unimportant, one way or the other.

But how about the cross-pressure situations? Can the difficulties here be traced to the division of authority? If so, what distinguished these two factories from the other four where cross-pressure did not develop to a noticeable extent?

The explanation appears to be that there were two conditions present in these factories which, combined with the division of authority, made the relationships difficult. First, in both instances, the factory manager feared the potential power of the controller's department more than he valued the accounting service. In his eyes, the controller's department constituted a threat to his managerial prerogatives. He foresaw a danger to his own authority in reporting detailed accounting information to the company offices. Second (and considerable importance is attached to this point), in both instances the controller's department received little support from the company manufacturing executives in its efforts to increase attention-directing services at the factory.

This latter point is a bit paradoxical, for it might be expected that the factory manager's resistance to having accounting reports flow back to the home office would be increased as pressure was exerted on him by the company manufacturing executives who received the reports. But this is not supported by the evidence. In the two cross-pressure situations, the absence of pressure from company manufacturing executives using accounting data led the factory manager to view the accountant's activity as an unnecessary and undesirable encroachment on the manufacturing department.[5]

Thus, it appears that divided authority may create difficulties for the factory accountant if, (a) the factory manager is resistive to the controller's department, and (b) the controller's department is not supported by company manufacturing executives. Cross-pressures do not develop when *either one* of these conditions is absent. This conclusion must be held with some caution. First, it is based on observations in a very small number of factories. Second, no situations were encountered with centralized authority over the factory accountant where the same two conditions were operative. Hence, survey data do not show what the outcome would be if the line of formal authority ran directly and entirely from factory accountant to company controller. Presumably there would be at least one difference — if the factory accountant's loyalties lay entirely with the controller's department, the resistance of the factory manager would be less damaging to the morale of the factory accounting personnel.

The survey team's thinking on this point has been set forth at length because there has been much disagreement among writers on administration and among practicing managers on the essentiality of unity of command. Until further studies can be made on this point, the evidence cited here indicates that a division of formal authority over the factory accountant is entirely workable, provided that the controller's department has acceptance and support of company manufacturing executives. A man *can* serve two masters provided that the two masters are not working at cross purposes.

Asked if he thought it fair to have two bosses, one of the factory accountants

[5] This does not imply that the manufacturing vice president did not supervise factory operations in these two cases — in fact, the supervision was quite close. The point is that accounting data played a very slight role in the supervision, and were little used by the company manufacturing executives for attention-directing purposes.

who was operating very effectively under a system of decentralized, divided authority summed it up this way:

"Well, it's not easy. But if you prove sincerely that you're right and they recognize it, then you don't have too much difficulty. However, if you go one way or the other you might run into trouble in case of disputes between the company and the plant manager."

But this same factory accountant did not want to change to a centralized arrangement:

"Do you think there is any advantage in being under the direct supervision of the factory manager?"

"We help the factory management meet its responsibility to operate economically. But we only take orders from the home office as they relate to accounting policies."

Delegation of authority to the factory accountant. Thus far we have been considering the *relative* amount of authority exercised over the factory accountant by company controller and factory manager, respectively. A separate point is the amount of leeway allowed the factory accountant by the company controller's department to run his own shop. Whether authority was centralized or decentralized, it was found that the greatest service was being rendered to factory management when the factory accountant felt that he had authority to provide reports to the factory management as requested, within the minimum standards of accounting procedure and uniformity laid down by the controller's department.

The fear is sometimes expressed that, if the factory accountant is given this discretion, reports will multiply and accounting costs will grow out of all reason. Although it was expressed in one or two interviews, the majority of interviews and independent observation on this study do not provide grounds for this fear. Factory executives were quite modest in their requests for additional reports and were generally quite conscious of accounting costs. Several cases were observed where a factory manager actually requested discontinuance of specific reports he did not find useful.

All evidence indicates that there is much to be gained, for increased acceptance and effective use of accounting service, if the factory accountant is given the greatest possible leeway in adapting reports to local needs. Where this discretion is granted, control of accounting costs can be secured through the budget of the factory accounting department. Moreover, from time to time the controller, the factory manager and the factory accountant can review together local needs with reference to the report structure. Uniformity of accounting practices can be maintained through the chart of accounts and established procedures, a systematically planned report structure, internal audit, and a requirement that the factory accountant inform the home office accounting department of need for major changes in procedures and of local reports. Prior approval, except of major changes, does not appear essential.

Appointment of the factory accountant. Whatever the formal arrangements, the appointment and removal of factory accountants is almost always a matter of negotiation and agreement between the controller and the factory manager. The factory accountants were quite aware of this even though they looked to the controller's department for promotion.

84

Admitting this joint responsibility as an essential feature of the relationship, there is probably some advantage in placing the formal power of appointment in the controller's department. Such an arrangement establishes, in the minds of all concerned, the "right" of the controller's department to move men from one position to another. It facilitates the development of a group of trained executives in the controller's department. For the same reason, there may be some advantage in leaving salary administration for factory accounting personnel in the hands of the controller's department. No strong views were encountered on this point. Nor was there much concrete evidence as to the consequences of alternative arrangements. But the weight of opinion was on the side of vesting the controller's department with responsibility for these functions. As we shall see in a later section, the same opinions were expressed more strongly with reference to sales accounting.

Communications Channels Between Factory and Home Office

The problem of unity of command has another facet. The aspect of the problem considered in this section lies entirely within the controller's department. How shall communications between control and accounting units of the home office and the factory accounting department be channeled? Who in the home office shall be permitted to request services from, and give directions to, the factory accounting department?

All surveyed factory accounting departments received numerous requests for information and numerous instructions from the home office. The most important in terms of frequency and the amount of work involved for the factory were:

> Information requested for special studies being made by the company controller's department.
>
> Requests for cost data from company accounting or sales personnel concerned with pricing.
>
> Instructions to make specified changes in procedures.
>
> Instructions for changes in basic standards, usually resulting from changes in wages or material prices.
>
> Requests for specific information, especially in relation to billing of orders or to fuller explanation of variances.

Of course, all these are in addition to the flow of periodic accounting reports prepared at the factory and sent to the company home offices. Inquiries arising from reports of internal auditors are also excluded.

Inspection of the list shows that the requests and instructions originate from a number of different units in the home office controller's department. These include special studies units, pricing units, procedures and general accounting units, cost planning units, invoicing and accounts receivable units, and current analysis units. In each of the companies studied, there were at least two or three distinct organizational units in the home offices — and usually more — which had occasion for frequent contact with the factory accounting departments.

Several organizational questions are raised by these contacts. To what extent should instructions and requests be channeled through the factory accountant? Should there be a central focus point in the home office controller's department through which these communications are channeled? To what extent should information which is sent to the company offices be brought to the attention of the factory manager? What problems of work priorities are created for the factory accounting department, and how should these be handled?

Clearance with factory accountant. In most of the companies, requests and instructions from the home office to the factory accounting department are supposed (formally) to be transmitted through the factory accountant. This formal requirement tends to be honored more in the breach than in the observance, particularly in the case of requests for specific information. Informal relations grow up between personnel at both ends of the communication chain — they know whom to call or write for specific information, and they are unconvinced that there is any particular value in going through "channels." This is particularly true in the larger companies where there is considerable specialization among the accounting units at both company and factory offices.

We conclude that the practice of sending the factory accountant "information" copies of written requests for data, and of replies to such requests, is a more realistic procedure than requiring that all such communication be through the factory accountant. Initial clearance with the factory accountant should be necessary only on matters requiring considerable time on the part of factory accounting personnel.

The communications between home office and factory appear to operate most smoothly when the controller's department and the factory accounting department are organized in a more or less parallel fashion. Then the special studies unit in the home office has its main contact with the special studies unit in the factory; general accounting in the home office with general accounting in the factory, and so on. Under these circumstances, the factory accounting personnel do not come to feel that they are being buffeted by requests and demands from many sources in the home office, each clamoring for a top priority. If the organization plans recommended in this chapter and the preceding one are followed, such paralleling of units will be accomplished.

General supervisor of factory accounting. In six of the seven companies, a single executive in the company controller's department had primary responsibility for coordinating relationships between the home office and the factory accounting departments. In two companies, this was among the responsibilities of an assistant controller.

Four companies made such supervision a full-time responsibility of an executive in the controller's department. In one of the four companies, this executive spent most of his time in the field visiting factory accounting departments.

The seventh company did not have formal assignment of this responsibility. But the head of the internal audit unit gave particular attention to factory accounting problems.

In none of the companies was there insistence that all communications with the factories should be transmitted through the home office executives who supervised them. There was a tacit acknowledgement that such a procedure was both unnecessary and unworkable.

In the four cases where there was a general supervisor of factory accounting, he performed two main kinds of functions. First, he gave considerable attention to personnel matters — particularly the selection, promotion and transfer of top-ranking personnel in the factory accounting departments. Second, the supervisor of factory accounting often acted as a kind of buffer for the factory accounting departments. When competing claims were made on factory accounting departments by home office units, he attempted to act as representative of factory accountants and to "umpire" the dispute. When the factory accountants thought that deadlines were too tight, or that they needed budget increases, they turned to him as their representative at court.

In general, the supervisor of factory accounting appeared to be more successful and effective in his personnel management tasks than in his umpiring job. The umpiring arrangement, instead of reducing pressure and confusion, tended to add another party to the dispute.

In those cases where an assistant company controller supervised both factory accounting and general accounting, the assistant controller was not merely an intermediary between the factory controller and the company offices. The assistant controller was in a position to handle problems involving coordination between general company accounting and the factory since he had responsibility for both functions. This arrangement appeared to work more effectively than establishing a separate supervisory position for factory accounting.

General supervision over factory accounting can be exercised most effectively by the company controller or an assistant controller who also has responsibility for general accounting activities in the central offices.

Survey observations suggest additional recommendations to secure smooth working relations between the factory and the home office:

A strong factory accountant, who is given broad responsibility for running his department, will be his own effective representative at court if he has direct access to the company controller or an assistant controller. When conflicting demands are made on his personnel, he can first negotiate directly with the home office units involved. If this does not solve the problem (and observations indicate that it usually did) then he can have recourse to the company controller or assistant controller. In a number of the factories this kind of arrangement was operating very satisfactorily for all concerned.

Where the home office demands create repeated conflict for the factory accounting department, the problem calls for general policy changes rather than an *ad hoc* decision each time it arises. Sometimes a rearrangement of the timetable for periodic reports to the home office would remove the difficulty. In other cases the factory accounting department may have insufficient staff, and a budget decision has to be reached, either to reduce the work load by eliminating requests or to increase the budget. Neither of these solutions would seem to require an intermediary between the factory accountant and the company controller or his assistant.

The parallel arrangement of organization units, already mentioned, facilitates agreement on the budget requirements of the factory accounting department because it makes it relatively easy to isolate and measure the work load that is created in the factory by the various home office units.

The conclusion that a general supervisor of factory accounting is not needed is advanced only after careful consideration because it is contrary to the arrangement now in force in the majority of the companies studied, and because at least two of the companies, after experience with both plans, have established this position. Nevertheless the survey team is in agreement that the facts developed in interviews and by observation do not support the arguments in favor of the general supervisor of factory accounting.

The central question is whether, without establishing this position, the company controller can keep adequate contact with, and control over, the factory accounting units. This leads to several subsidiary questions.

If this position is not established, how will the company controller get the information he needs about the competence and effectiveness of the factory controllers? The answer, in the companies without this position, is that he gets it partly from the factory manager, and partly from the other company accounting executives — the internal auditor, the supervisor of general accounting, and the supervisor of cost control and analysis — all of whom have considerable contact with the factory.

How will the company controller secure adoption, at all factories, of improved procedures and practices developed at one factory? Won't the self-satisfaction of the factory accountants and rivalry among them prevent the ready interchange and acceptance of ideas unless someone with authority in the home office can implement them? Again, observations do not indicate that this potential difficulty was actually realized in the companies operating without a general supervisor of factory accounting.

Relations with the factory manager. Where the factory manager has formal administrative authority over the factory accountant, a strict adherence to unity of command would require all communications to the factory accounting department to be transmitted through the factory manager. Actual practice observed made it evident that there is even less justification for this arrangement than for the requirement that the factory accountant be the sole channel of communication.

The distinction between "administrative" matters and "technical accounting" matters was sufficiently well understood in companies with decentralized authority so that no confusion resulted from by-passing the factory manager. It is clear that any potential difficulties can be anticipated and avoided by sending the factory manager copies of important requests and instructions.

The same recommendation applies to communications with the home office. Most of the companies were quite careful to see that accounting information, relating to factory operations, was not sent to the home office without informing the factory manager and supplying him with a copy of the data. The main reason for this — and an important reason — is to prepare the factory manager for any inquiries that may come from his superiors as a result of the information supplied to them. It is essential that the factory accounting department remove any suspicion from the factory manager's mind that the accountants are "spies" for the company management.

RECAPITULATION: FACTORY ACCOUNTING

In the preceding sections, a general scheme has been suggested for organization of the factory accounting department. Omitting qualifications, the main recommendations are:

Separating analytical functions from record-keeping functions.

Centralizing at the factory level the location and supervision of cost planning, special studies, and record keeping; decentralizing current analysis to departments or groups of departments.

Strengthening the position of the factory accountant by giving him broad administrative responsibility and direct access to the company controller or assistant controller.

As far as possible, establishing accounting and control units with parallel functions at company and factory levels, and permitting and encouraging direct communication between counterpart units at the two levels.

Keeping the number of levels in the accounting organization at a minimum by avoiding, in general, the establishment of the position (at the company level) of general supervisor of factory accounting, or the position (at the factory level) of supervisor of departmental accounting units.

As far as formal authority is concerned, both centralized and decentralized arrangements have been found to be workable. With authority over the factory accountant divided between the company controller and the factory manager, the accounting services must be given real support, both at the company and at the factory level of the manufacturing department. If this cannot be guaranteed, centralization of authority in the hands of the company controller may be preferable to decentralization.

ACCOUNTING AND CONTROL FOR SALES FUNCTIONS

The report on organization of sales accounting can be relatively brief. The data-collecting problems are less complex than in the manufacturing area, the reports are simpler, and survey observations suggest that, at least for attention-directing purposes, greater reliance can be placed upon the operating personnel to take responsibility for analysis of the data. Three common characteristics of sales department operations in these companies have an important bearing on the organization problem.

First, the sales function is usually widely dispersed on a geographical basis with a large number of offices, each with relatively few employees. Often there are several layers of geographically dispersed units — company operated branches (in several of the companies), district offices, and regional offices.

Second, it is seldom possible to arrive at direct measures of efficiency in sales operations. It is possible to measure the volume of sales and to measure the marketing costs, but it is far more difficult than in manufacturing — indeed, generally impossible — to find a direct relation between the cost of sales effort and the results produced by it. This means that reporting the facts is a relatively straightforward job, but that the interpretation of the facts rests primarily with the sales executives. Variance analysis and the principle of exceptions may help to indicate when operations are costly, but they are not very helpful as indications of efficiency.

Third, there is less of a barrier to communication between accountants and sales executives than between accountants and manufacturing executives. Sales executives are generally less resistive to using figures than manufacturing executives are. This is true partly because it is impossible to observe directly the work of each salesman. The accounting personnel, too, find it easier to familiarize themselves with the "technology" of the marketing side of the business than with the technology of the factory.

Accounting Service Functions for Sales

The questions here are similar to those discussed in previous chapters. At what levels in the organization is accounting service needed? What are the effective ways of developing communications channels? Are the levels at which attention-directing data are needed the same as the levels at which problem-solving data are needed?

Attention-directing services. In these companies, the main data used by the sales executives for attention-directing purposes are figures on sales, classified by product and by territory, and figures on the expenditures of the various units in the sales department. The same types of data, with varying amounts of detail in classification, are needed by virtually all executives in the sales organization, regardless of rank.

Even where standards are established in the form of sales quotas, sales executives express a strong preference for actual sales figures rather than variance from standards. Whether or not quotas are established, sales executives have their own mental standards based on daily scrutiny of sales figures and on salesmen's reports of the volume of sales which a territory or district can be expected to produce. They are interested not only in the comparison of actual sales with quotas, but with previous sales, with share of market, and with over-all trends in the company, the industry, and general business conditions. They are continually using the "principle of exceptions" based on such comparisons to locate trouble spots. In these companies at least, survey results point to the conclusion that sales executives have relatively little need for help from accounting department personnel in this kind of current analysis. The matter of long-term trends and problems, however, is a somewhat different situation and is discussed in greater detail on page 92.

No matter where the formal sales reports are prepared — whether at centralized or decentralized locations — the data generally originate at the point of sale, and the local sales personnel usually keep "black books" of approximate sales figures that are much more current than those the accounting department can provide. Accounting figures serve primarily to give the composite picture as a check on the longer run trends, and as a basis for more detailed analysis of specific products. For this reason, the centralized compilation of sales reports by the accounting department does not interfere with use of the data, provided that these are transmitted back to regional and district offices with reasonable promptness. Clerical economy and a sufficient degree of geographical centralization to gain the advantages of specialization and mechanization would appear to be the ruling considerations in determining the organization level at which such reports should be prepared.

A similar conclusion was reached on reports of sales department expenditures. The sales department, unlike the manufacturing department, ordinarily operates on a fixed budget. The primary use of the budget reports is to determine whether the local sales unit is keeping within the budgeted expenditures. Since the principal items of expenditure are relatively stable, and since salary and wage costs can be controlled by watching the size of staff, these reports do not have the same urgency as in the manufacturing department. For these reasons, the reports should be compiled at levels where this can be done economically. This usually implies a considerable degree of geographical centralization.

A few comments are in order as to the use made by sales executives of the internal audit reports on district offices and company-operated branches. In several cases, the sales executives regarded the audit reports as the most valuable information received from the accounting department — more useful than the sales and budget reports. Here is a typical comment:

"How do you judge which districts are well run?"

"Partly, we judge that by analysis of reports and partly by personal observation — getting down and meeting the district managers."

"What reports are particularly useful in judging them?"

"Well, for example, just a couple of weeks ago I received an audit report. The auditor gave a very glowing account about the office. I noticed on the audit report that the district's sales exceeded anything in that region. I made a note of this and as soon as I get a chance I'm going to ask why."

"Is the audit report the main source you use in judging the districts?"

"We also look at the expenses. My assistant (in the sales department) analyzes these for me every month and points out districts that are exceptionally good or bad. We often pick up valuable selling ideas this way."

"How often do you find something in an audit report that you follow up?"

"I suppose I write two or three letters a month from things I get out of the audit reports."

Special studies. Almost all the questions that call for the problem-solving use of accounting data in sales management are company-level problems. The main categories of such problems are: setting prices, identifying profitable and unprofitable items and branch locations, and developing effective merchandising methods and channels.

Except for the use of cost data to price customers' orders, regular periodic accounting reports were almost never used for problem-solving purposes in these areas. The reasons have been stated in general terms in Chapter 3, page 36 and pages 38 ff. But in order to understand more clearly how the accounting department can aid the decision-making process, let us carry through in some detail a rather typical example of profitability analysis, drawn from the National Supply Company. Comparable problems were found in every one of the companies we studied.

The National Supply Company operates retail branches that sell oil field supplies to drillers and operators. Because oil-producing districts rise and decline rapidly, the sales executives are faced with decisions as to when to open and close sales branches. Much of the drilling activity is carried on by large national oil companies.

The company's periodic accounting reports show, on a monthly basis, the profit or loss for each sales branch. There are some intricate accounting problems in developing these profit and loss figures. Sales must be allocated to the branches. This is sometimes difficult when customers have central purchasing operations. A policy must be established for determining the cost to the branches of goods manufactured in the company's own factories. Company overhead must be allocated.

But these are not the central problems with which we are now concerned. Suppose that all the questions of accounting procedure can be settled to the satisfaction of everyone concerned. The main problem of how to decide when to open or close a sales branch still remains. In a new oil field it may be necessary to open a branch long before there is a profitable volume of business in order to obtain customers before they have formed the habit of patronizing competitors. Similarly, a branch in a declining field may be kept open when it is no longer profitable — at least in the accounting reckoning — in order to continue to give service to customers who are operating in other fields as well. There is no way in which the value of customer relations can be shown on the books of account.

Clearly, decisions to open or close sales branches are going to depend largely on extensive analysis and forecasting, combined with the judgment of the sales executives. Profit, as reported on the periodic accounting statements, is not going to be a ruling criterion. To supplement executive judgment by more objective analysis would call for careful research to determine how the success of the company in securing business in a new field depends on the timing of opening branches; to determine the area from which branches can draw customers; and to determine how much the company's business depends on a reputation for service.

Such a study might well require various kinds of "external" data — obtained from market surveys and trade statistics — as well as careful analysis of internal operating and accounting records of past operations. But accounting data needed in such an investigation would have to be provided on a special "one-shot" basis rather than through periodic reports.

A solution to the problem of providing special analyses in the merchandising area of large companies would be to assign this function to a small unit in the company controller's department. The unit would not have the task of preparing periodic reports, but would be charged with the responsibility of developing close contacts with the market research unit, if there is one, and with the top sales executives. Several approximations to this arrangement were found in the companies studied, but no instance where the special studies work did not tend to be somewhat overshadowed by the preparation of periodic reports. In smaller companies, of course, a single unit might have responsibility for special studies in both the sales and manufacturing areas.

In most of the companies studied, the cost of such a special analysis group could be absorbed by reducing the volume of periodic accounting reports provided to sales executives and not used by them. In this category the survey team would place most of the detailed reports on product profitability. These are inevitably based on average-costing principles with full distribution of overhead, and therefore, not very satisfactory for important marketing decisions.

RECORD-KEEPING FUNCTIONS

In sales accounting, the operations involving the greatest volume of clerical work are billing and maintenance of accounts receivable. Since these functions involve the credit and manufacturing operations as well as sales, their organization has been discussed in Chapter 4, pages 65 ff. The conclusions reached there were that, for reasons of access, it is usually advantageous to locate accounts receivable in the same cities as the credit units; that there is no particular need, for reasons of promptness, to decentralize geographically; and that from a cost standpoint, a considerable measure of geographical centralization is desirable.

There appear to be few problems of access that cannot be solved by making carbon copies of important source documents. For example, with centralized report preparation, it is probably common practice to keep copies of the initial sales records in the local sales offices. Some duplication of stock and inventory records may be unavoidable when the actual stocks of goods are held in a number of locations. But this is not necessarily so. If the number of different items held in inventory is small, this creates no serious difficulty or great cost. But if there is a large number of items, the annual valuation of inventories may create a serious peak load for a centralized unit responsible for pricing the quantity lists. This has been solved in one company by providing the warehouses and other inventory points with a standard price list to be used in inventory valuation so that all steps except the final compilation can be performed locally. Where this is done, the classification scheme for the central inventory records does not have to be as elaborate as the stock classification.

Where there are a number of echelons in the sales organization — for example, stores or sales branches with or without stocks, districts, regions, and company office — nothing appears to be gained by paralleling this structure in the accounting organization. At most, an accounting unit might be needed where invoices are prepared and stock records maintained, where there are credit and collections units (say, the regional office) and at the home office. Data flowing upward can, with economy, simply by-pass intermediate levels which will require at most an office manager to be responsible for accounting functions on a part-time basis.

ORGANIZATION STRUCTURE

As in the case of manufacturing operations, the decentralized sales accounting personnel can report directly and solely to the company controller's department (centralized authority) or can be responsible administratively to the sales office, functionally to the controller's department (decentralized authority). In general, companies which centralize the authority over the factory controller, also centralize authority over sales accounting personnel; and those which decentralize authority in the one case also do so in the other.

The supervisors of geographically decentralized sales accounting units frequently have the title of "office manager," and just as frequently have duties that relate as much to personnel, general office supervision and merchandising as to accounting. For this reason they are more likely than are the factory accountants to regard themselves, and to be regarded, as members of the operating executive's staff. A significant index of this difference is revealed in the many instances found where sales accounting personnel had been promoted to other sales positions, but almost a complete absence of instances (except in one company) where factory accounting personnel had been promoted to operating positions. On the whole, the case for decentralized authority appears stronger in the sales than in the manufacturing area.

Whether it is desirable for the controller to retain the authority to appoint and transfer office managers hinges to a certain degree on where their promotional opportunities lie. Where the normal lines of personnel movement lie *within* the controller's department, the office managers themselves tend to prefer to have personnel and salary administration in the hands of the controller's department. They believe that because of the sales executives' interests and concerns, sales personnel are likely to be better treated in salary matters than they are, and that they are apt to find themselves in dead-end positions.

Chapter 6

THE DEVELOPMENT OF ACCOUNTING PERSONNEL

The final criterion in appraising the controller's organization is its effect on the development of personnel. Most executives would willingly sacrifice some short-run efficiency if, by doing so, they could contribute substantially to the training and development of potential supervisors and executives in their organization. Hence, it is necessary to ask whether the organizational patterns that recommend themselves on the basis of economy, or immediate effectiveness of accounting service, are also adequately effective for personnel development.

To test the potential of an organization for developing personnel, attention was given to normal channels of promotion to determine whether these are designed to give men well-rounded and progressively responsible experience. The main skills to be developed through this experience are:

Ability to manage and supervise the work of others.

Broad accounting knowledge and imaginative understanding of the uses of accounting data.

Understanding of the major operating problems in production, sales, and finance.

Ability to view these problems from an integrated, company-wide viewpoint.

EFFECTS OF CONTROLLER'S ORGANIZATION STRUCTURE ON PERSONNEL DEVELOPMENT

There are two ways in which the form of organization affects the kinds of experience to which men are exposed in their careers. First, organization structure determines the combinations of abilities and skills needed in particular positions. Second, organization structure tends to influence the normal lines of promotion.

In most organizations, promotion tends to be more or less "vertical." When a position is vacant, the initial reaction is to fill it by promotion from one of the positions immediately subordinate to it, or from a neighboring part of the organization. From a short-run standpoint, the path of least resistance is to find a man whose previous experience will permit him to take over the job with a minimum of training and new learning. For example, it is "natural" to replace the chief factory accountant by promoting his assistant, or by transferring a man from a smaller factory to a larger one.

Effect of Separating Analysis from Record Keeping

If the organizational recommendations of earlier chapters are followed — particularly the recommendation that current analysis, special studies, and record keeping be performed by different units in the controller's organization — a vertical promotion policy is likely to lead to difficulties. Suppose, for example, that a man begins his career in a record-keeping unit. The "natural" lines of promotion will make him the supervisor of successively larger and more important record-keeping units. He may reach a responsible position — say, as assistant factory accountant or supervisor of general accounting and control. Such a man, while he may have acquired supervisory skill and a good knowledge of accounting procedures, has probably also acquired far too narrow an outlook about the managerial role of controllership functions to qualify him for the next steps in the executive ladder. Moreover, at this point in his career it is no longer easy to transfer him "side-wise" into a responsible analytical position.

The man who has risen on the analytical side of the organization is in the same difficulty. Since analytical units are generally small, he may well have reached a fairly high level in the unit without having had experience in supervising a large staff which operates on a "production" basis. The design of efficient clerical procedures and the management of a clerical staff may be largely unknown territory to him. At this point in his career he can hardly be made head of a small record-keeping unit solely for the purpose of giving him supervisory experience.

Perhaps, in order to state the problem clearly, the picture has been depicted too sharply in black and white. Actually it is likely to be made up of shades of gray. By accident, if not by design, the careers of most men are likely to deviate at some point from the straight line described above. It may be argued, too, that if a man has outstanding abilities, the fact that his experience has exposed him only to a limited portion of the controller's problems will not prevent him from learning his new responsibilities.

Granting all that, there is still no need to make a virtue out of necessity. It is no particular recommendation of an organization plan that the problems of executive development can be solved in spite of it. It should not be left to accident to provide rounded experience for potential executives. Nor is an organization safe in relying on the occasional man of outstanding ability, who is able to succeed on a job for which his previous experience has not prepared him adequately. Hence, the research team would have serious reservations about the organization plans proposed in the earlier chapters if they interfered with executive training objectives.

It is our judgment that the separation of the analytical from the record-keeping functions need not interfere with executive development, provided that an intelligent and carefully administered plan is instituted for the horizontal transfer of potential supervisors and executives at several stages in their careers. "Horizontal transfer" means promotion from analytical positions to supervisory positions in record-keeping units, and vice versa.

This recommendation can be made more specific by seeing how it is accomplished in one of the factories studied. In this factory, college-trained accounting personnel generally begin in junior analytical positions. Before a man is promoted beyond the position of senior cost analyst, the factory controller watches for an opportunity to give him a tour of duty as section head of a cost accounting unit or the stores accounting unit, or in some similar position. When he has had such experience, the man can be promoted to a more responsible position involving either

96

analysis or supervision. If he moves upward along one of these lines, another opportunity can be found later in his career to transfer him "sidewise" again at a middle-management level. The head of the general accounting unit in the factory, for example, might be transferred to be head of cost planning and analysis. The more varied the experience the man has had in the earlier stages of his career, the easier it is to continue to give him varied assignments at the later stages.

The key to the whole procedure lies in not permitting a man to advance very long in one specialized aspect of controllership. Advancement should be coupled with lateral transfer. No very elaborate machinery is needed to accomplish this. Somewhere in the organization there needs to be a list of men who are good prospects for promotion. When a vacancy occurs, instead of following the "natural" process of vertical promotion, the list can be reviewed to see what men are available for the position, and what their needs are for further training and experience.

The best evidence of the feasibility of an executive development plan of this kind is that it is being carried on, and carried on successfully, in several of the companies studied. In those companies the separation of analytical activities from record-keeping activities did not interfere with the development of potential executives for the top positions in the controller's organization.

Geographical Decentralization and Development of Effective Managers

The geographical decentralization of accounting personnel to factories and regional offices may have two potential effects — one favorable and one unfavorable — upon executive development. The favorable effect is that it creates responsible field positions where a man is more or less "on his own," and where he can learn to run an organization without close supervision. The unfavorable effect is that decentralization may make it difficult to provide an adequate variety of experience, except by moving men from one city to another. This problem is apt to be most serious in sales accounting because of the small size of units in each location.

Factory chief accountants and divisional controllers generally were found to be self-reliant and to have good administrative abilities, plus a relatively broad managerial outlook. To be sure, one of the reasons they were appointed to these positions was that they were thought to possess such qualities. Hence, it cannot be cited as direct, conclusive evidence of the training value of the positions. But, in terms of the skills required of the factory accountant or divisional controller, and the opportunities he has to gain broad experience, there is every reason to regard his position as an excellent one for developing top executives. The position of assistant factory controller also appears to provide broader and more responsible experience than most positions at the same level in company offices.

The position of office manager in a regional or district sales office has less to offer from a training standpoint than factory accounting positions. As has been pointed out in previous chapters, there is less possibility in sales than in manufacturing for decentralizing analytical services, and the office manager has less leeway in the reports he can prepare for the sales department.

Where the duties of the office manager are not restricted to accounting, but take him into other aspects of the work of the sales office, he has greater opportunities to acquire useful and broadening experience. This adds additional weight to the possibility suggested in the last chapter, namely, finding some promotional opportunities for office managers in the sales department so that they will have a real incentive to learn about merchandising and to serve as members of the sales manager's administrative team.

SOME TRAINING PROBLEMS IN THE ACCOUNTING DEPARTMENT

The horizons of the accounting and controllership professions have widened steadily over recent years, so that these professions now conceive their primary functions to include provision of a wide range of data-reporting, data-analyzing and consultative services for management. How far can the day-to-day experience of accounting personnel be relied on to give the insight and knowledge needed to realize these broader conceptions of the controllership function? Does the concept which the accountant forms of his job depend at all upon the organization structure? Do the different forms of organization for the controller's department facilitate or hinder the accountant in acquiring skills and knowledge that are involved in analytical work? If any definite relationships were found between the organization structure and on-the-job learning in these areas, considerable weight would have to be given to these relationships in reaching decisions about organization. The survey team's principal findings on this point are briefly stated in the following paragraphs.

The decentralization of analytical services and the development of close communication with operating personnel have a substantial impact on the way in which accountants think about their jobs. Usually the men who have had close contact with operations have acquired an appreciation of the operating executive's problems and some idea about how the operating man can and cannot use accounting data. That their understanding on the latter point is often still short of a desirable goal has been reported in Chapter 3. In spite of these shortcomings, the decentralized organization, with well-developed horizontal communication channels, appears to have proved its usefulness as an educational device.

While decentralization widens the horizons of the accountant and gives him a broader view of his function, it is less successful in providing him with the tools needed to carry out this broader function. Unless his training enables him to do otherwise, he will still approach his analytical tasks with the traditional tools of his profession. The cost analysts interviewed and observed in this study ranged from unusual competence and ability to mediocrity. Within this range of abilities, many of the weaknesses encountered could be traced back to narrowness of basic training and experience. These weaknesses are exemplified by many of the analytical personnel who devote too much time and effort to routine reports, credit cost standards and variances with a greater objectivity and validity than the standards commonly possess, ignore the distinction between real savings and "wooden money" savings, cost on an average basis rather than on an incremental or variable basis, and fail to use adequate methods of statistical analysis. Furthermore, a substantial number of these people in accounting and control are deficient in fundamental knowledge of the technological problems and market structure of their company and their industry. When found, deficiencies of these kinds were commonly associated with a narrow concept of the controllership function and with a lack of fundamental training.

In conclusion, therefore, many of the potential advantages of decentralization, in the sense of broadening the accounting functions, will be realized only if personnel are adequately prepared to exploit these advantages. It should be noted that this conclusion is less a criticism of accounting personnel than of the professional training and experience pattern which has produced them. The less able among the analysts have perhaps learned too well the traditional accounting techniques, and have had too little opportunity to acquire the other fundamental tools essential for good analysis and competence in control functions. Few of the analysts interviewed, for example, have mastered the techniques of cost comparison studies at the level of the standard introductory textbooks in that subject.

Pre-entry Training

The deficiency just noted in the analytical skills of many accounting personnel is not likely to be removed by changes in organization structure. Men often acquire relatively specific and narrow skills from on-the-job experience; they seldom acquire broad fundamental knowledge, techniques and broad points of view in this way. This is an important reason for transferring responsibility for fundamental training from industry to the colleges — a shift that has been taking place steadily in our society for several generations and that shows no signs of halting.

This shift is not peculiar to the accounting profession. It is even more clearly visible, for example, in engineering. Two generations ago, most engineers in industry were "practical" engineers who had started at the drafting board and had learned engineering on the job. Few practical engineers acquired in this way the kind of basic scientific and mathematical knowledge that has become more and more essential in important design work. For this reason, the college-trained engineer has largely taken over the fields of product development and design, and is moving rapidly into adjacent areas of activity.

In the light of this experience in other professions, this finding — that accountants do not easily acquire on the job the fundamental knowledge that is required for analytical work — should not be particularly surprising. Under any reasonable division of labor between the universities and industry in present-day society, the main responsibility for education in these *fundamental* points of view, analytical and management skills, must be assigned to pre-employment training rather than on-the-job experience. This is not to imply that nothing can be accomplished in this area by in-service training programs. Indeed, from a short-run standpoint, in-service training offers the only real possibility for broadening and deepening the understanding and skills of those persons now engaged in analysis who have not had this broader training prior to their employment. The real distinction is between the things a man is likely to learn from actual job experience and the things he is likely to learn only if he is exposed to formal training.

Let us be a bit more specific as to the nature of these preinduction training needs as they were revealed by study of analytical services. One of them — cost comparisons between alternative products and methods — has been mentioned. What the accountant needs is the basic theory and practical techniques for making an economic comparison between alternative courses of action in order to determine which is the more profitable. The techniques are based on a few fairly simple ideas: a thorough understanding of the meaning of interest costs on capital expenditures; selection of the appropriate interest rate for calculations and avoidance of the dangers of double-counting; understanding of the economic, as well as the accounting, meanings of depreciation and obsolescence; understanding of the economic meaning of fixed and variable costs. Other items could be added, but these are the central concepts involved.

A second area of importance is the economics of price determination. The common distrust in sales departments of accounting analyses of product profitability has already been noted. If cost data are to be used as a basis for pricing special orders, much economic sophistication is needed in their preparation. Daily contact with customers and markets tends to impress rather forcibly upon sales executives some of the basic facts of economic life. Accountants are at least one stage removed from this direct contact and have a corresponding need for more formal training in the economic effects of pricing policies and product-line policies.

A third area is statistics. When the accountant enters the area of special studies, his problem is more often one of estimating future data than of compiling historical figures. Although there are numerous signs of change, traditional accounting training is still generally weak in the theory and technique of estimating and forecasting. Adequate basic training for controllership or managerial accounting should include some acquaintance with modern techniques for making business and market forecasts, and their applications to the problems of a company, and some appreciation of the uses of nonaccounting data obtained from outside sources and from market research.

A fourth area is methods analysis and production control, as these are viewed by the industrial engineer. The responsibilities of the accounting department and the industrial engineering department for setting standards are closely interrelated. For effective cooperation between the two groups, each needs to go more than half way in learning about the techniques of the other.

In earlier chapters, the conclusion was reached that decentralization of analytical services, at least to the factory level, will generally lead to an improvement in controllership service. Facts and analysis presented in this chapter indicate that the potential advantages of decentralization are likely to be realized to the extent that controllers' departments are able to recruit personnel having had the requisite fundamental training outlined in preceding paragraphs.

Further broadening in the training of industrial accountants is essential if the profession is to reach its goal of making the controller and his staff full-fledged partners in the management team, if controllership is not to be limited largely to its financial and record-keeping aspects. Unless a continuing supply of well-trained personnel is provided, the primary responsibility for interpreting reports, making current analyses, and undertaking special studies will tend to gravitate to other departments of the company, for example, special staff units reporting to top executives or to the industrial engineering department which already carries on part of the analytical work.

PROMOTIONS ACROSS DEPARTMENTAL LINES

The problems of personnel development are too narrowly conceived if the controller's department is viewed in complete isolation from other parts of the company. Survey observations suggest that some of the difficulties reported in securing close relations between the controller's department and the operating departments are partially eliminated where there has been a fair amount of interchange of personnel. This is particularly true in the area of special studies. Since special analyses frequently require the technical contributions of several professions, good analytical work is harder to secure in organizations where personnel are highly specialized than in organizations where they have been exposed to a variety of experience.

A number of the controllers in the companies studied are clearly aware of the advantages which might be secured through such interchange. They do not, however, always find it easy to bring this about. Frequently, they find it difficult to compete with other departments for personnel with adequately broad training. Most of the companies, for example, were eager to appoint to factory accounting positions some men who had combined engineering and accounting training. In some cases they found that the prevailing salaries for engineers were substantially higher than the controller's department salary scale. Even when this obstacle was absent, they found that the distinction between public accounting and industrial accounting was not widely understood, and that many of the men they would like to recruit consequently were not attracted to the industrial accounting profession.

These problems obviously go beyond the organizational questions with which this study is primarily concerned. However, a few suggestions are offered which were gleaned from the experience of three of the companies which had been relatively successful in attracting men to their controller's organizations.

The matter of setting an attractive salary scale is so obvious (even though it may not always be feasible) that it does not require further comment. Apart from salary, what appears to attract men with broad training to positions in the controller's department is a belief that this offers a chance to work closely with operating men, that such jobs will provide broad and progressively responsible experience over the range of the company's activities, and that they will have opportunities to advance *either* within the controller's department *or* in operating positions in the manufacturing or sales departments. In fact, in that company which has been the most successful of the seven in developing a broadly trained staff of cost analysts, advancement into the manufacturing department is one of the normal routes of promotion rather than an exceptional channel.

This observation points to another value of decentralized analytical services. While decentralization may not, by itself, provide the means for developing personnel in the basic nonaccounting skills, it may be very helpful in attracting to the organization men who already possess these skills. A successful company record of promotions across departmental lines may be the best concrete evidence for the prospective employee that the broad controllership function he is told about is an actuality and not merely a hope.

The development of interdepartmental promotional opportunities has a further consequence. It has already been mentioned that operating executives who have done accounting work at some point in their careers generally make considerably more use of accounting data than do executives in the same organization without such experience. The controller's department can make an important long-range contribution to its own effectiveness by feeding such men into the general organization or to the operating departments. In the companies where this has been done, the presence of men in the operating departments who had previous experience in accounting aided materially in securing effective horizontal communications.

In general, organizational units concerned with planning and with special studies afford the greatest opportunities for interdepartmental transfer of personnel. At the factory, some of the accounting personnel should be qualified, from time to time, to move into industrial engineering work. Several cases were found where this had occurred. In a large factory, a man with accounting experience might prove very useful in an assignment as a staff assistant to the factory manager. The engineering department offers possibilities for a man who has had both accounting and engineering training. In industries where the technology is not too involved, promotions into manufacturing line positions are sometimes feasible. This was fairly common practice in one of the surveyed companies.

As has been noted, movement of personnel from accounting to the sales department appears to occur fairly often. In the company home office, the market research unit might be an excellent spot for broadening the experience of an accounting man, at the same time injecting some accounting thinking into the marketing work. There is also the possibility of staffing units set up to make special studies of complex, extensive problems with teams drawn from several departments.

The promotion of men across departmental lines need not be a one-way proposition. The same considerations that make it advantageous to encourage some transfers and promotions from the controller's department to operating departments, hold also for movement in the opposite direction. To be sure, for a man to perform successfully in an accounting position, he must have a minimum of formal accounting training. But all the evidence indicates that the minimum required for good analytical work is not very great. Men of above-average ability with an understanding of production and the economics of business management can learn on the job if they have had some introduction to double entry accounting and cost accounting.

This conclusion is based on three kinds of evidence. First, a number of cases were found where men had been moved into accounting positions from other departments. Second, several of the companies recruit for analytical positions college graduates who have had a minimum of formal training in accounting. Third, experience at several schools of business administration indicates that, with about one year of accounting training, graduates with above-average records have sufficient fundamental knowledge of accounting to handle analytical work.

The comments made earlier about interunit transfers *within* the accounting department apply to interdepartmental transfers as well. Unless there is some deliberate planning for executive development, the horizontal movement of personnel will not come about naturally. If definite steps are taken to broaden the experience of men early in their careers, through horizontal transfers and by other means, this in turn makes easier similar moves at higher levels.

102

INTERDEPARTMENTAL TEAMS FOR SPECIAL STUDIES

In Chapter 4, pages 58 to 60, the question was raised as to how far the controller's department responsibilities should extend in the area of special studies. Two reasons were set forth as to why the responsibility must be shared jointly with the operating departments. The first was that only the operating departments would have a sufficient knowledge of all the merchandising and manufacturing problems involved in important policy questions. The second was that the kinds of problems that require formal analysis are so closely tied in with the operating functions that operating executives are unlikely to be willing to delegate to another department the major responsibility for developing recommendations.

There is another aspect to the question. A controller's department which followed the general kinds of recruitment, training, and promotion policies discussed in this chapter, could contribute much to the management planning which would precede decisions on selection of equipment, location of factories, addition or discontinuance of product lines, pricing of products. Part of this contribution can be made through the policies of interdepartmental promotion already described — by providing accounting experience for a number of men who later move into the operating departments.

In addition to this, there would seem to be a real place for temporary units, with staff assigned from several departments, as a device for undertaking major planning studies. Several instances were noted where this idea was used, principally in making studies on reporting and clerical procedures affecting other departments besides the controller's. In some other cases, informal groups had evolved, at the initiative of two or three individuals from different departments, who found themselves concerned with the same problem. In general, these companies had not developed any definite policies for the employment of interdepartmental teams. Where such teams had been created, they had been established to deal with some particular problem that had arisen.

There is no point, of course, in setting up interdepartmental analytical groups unless there is a problem requiring study. On the other hand, if the device has value — both as a means for getting better management planning and as a means for personnel development — it appears that advantage is not always being taken of the opportunities to use the device. Controllers' departments might well follow a definite policy of encouraging the establishment of interdepartmental units when important questions require study and of loaning to such special units, on temporary assignment, analytical personnel from the controller's department.

DEVELOPING A GENERAL MANAGEMENT VIEWPOINT

Throughout this chapter it has been apparent that the problems of developing accounting personnel cannot be dealt with entirely within the framework of the controller's department. They must be viewed in terms of the business organization as a whole. In concluding this study, the survey team should like to call attention to still another facet of the relationship between controllership organization and company general management. At each higher level in the management pyramid, the range of matters with which the executive is concerned broadens. To make good decisions he must secure the contributions of a wider and wider range of skills and professional techniques. To secure these contributions, the organization structure has to be adapted to the kinds of skills that society, through its professional and other training facilities, produces.

From this standpoint, organizing the controllership and accounting function is only partly a task of determining the role of *accounting* in business; it is equally a task of determining the role of the *accountant* in business. "Accounting" and "the accountant" are not necessarily synonymous, nor are they synonymous with "controller" and "controllership."

The industrial controllers interviewed in the course of this study are keenly aware of these broader managerial responsibilities. Like engineers, financial specialists, sales specialists, and other groups engaged in business, professional accountants and controllers want their activity to make its full contribution to the operation of their companies. They want to have their share of opportunities to participate in general management functions. The controllers are generally aware, too, that when top accounting executives begin to assume general management responsibilities, they need a broader point of view than the strictly departmental one provided by the technical accounting function.

It would be wrong to suppose that the accountant, merely by being an accountant, acquires a broader view of the company's problems than does the engineer, the lawyer, or the sales executive. The real contribution that the controller's department can make to the development of potential executives is to provide a channel — along with all the other professional channels — through which the company can attract, develop, and train intelligent, ambitious, and hard-working men. The value of the channel will depend on the kinds of men who come into the accounting profession, the kinds of business training they have, as well as their in-service training and experience.

Organization structure, by reflecting the structure of the professions, gives each profession in business its opportunity to participate in management. Long-range shifts in organization structure are often a consequence of the success that the various professions have had in demonstrating their competence to handle particular kinds of management problems. In this "struggle for existence," superior competence and training of the members of a profession are likely to lead to larger responsibilities for that profession in the long run. Even the most casual glance at industrial history reveals this rise and fall of professional groups and the emergence of new ones.

The conclusions reached by the survey team in this study as to the proper scope of the controllership function and the controller's department are conditioned by observations of the training and experience of the personnel now engaged in the industrial accounting profession. It is a relatively new profession which has only recently begun to formulate its goals and its educational needs. The limits of its functions and opportunities are not fixed for all time. What they will be, or ought to be, a generation hence will depend in considerable measure upon industrial accountants and controllers themselves — both the account they give of themselves as individuals, and what they are able to accomplish through their organized professional groups.

INDEX

ACCOUNTING
control, 64, 89
data, use of, 37, 45
department, training problems in, 98
factory, 88
functions, organization of, 66
information, flow of, 47
information, quality of, 63
operations, authority over, 8
personnel, development of, 9
problems, understanding of, 51
responsibility, 43
service functions, 90
supervision, factory organization of, 80, 86
ATTENTION DIRECTING
analysis, current, 74
organizing for, 45
"principle of exceptions," 26
services, 90
use of figures, 3
uses of data, 24
illustrations, 24
AUTHORITY
centralization and decentralization, 17
decentralized accounting operations, 8
delegation of, to factory accountant, 84

CENTRALIZATION AND DECENTRALIZATION
account structure, 4, 39
analysis, current, 5
authority, 17
communication, 19
controller's departments, 13
degree and elements, 14
geographical, 16
meaning, 1, 13
operating departments, 13
record keeping, 7
significance of operations, 19
studies, special, 6
COMMUNICATIONS
between factory and home office, 85
centralization and decentralization, 19
"horizontal," 48
implications for organization, 53

providing channels, 47
"vertical," 52
CONTROLLER'S DEPARTMENT
centralization and decentralization, 13
organization, 5, 69
participation, 58
COSTS
considerations, 60
control and standards, 73
production, comparisons, 35
record-keeping functions, 77

EASTMAN KODAK CO.
accounting employees in manufacturing departments, 19
credits and collections, 12
decentralization, degree of, 19, 20
factory accounting executive, 17
industrial engineer as controllership function, 13
organization, 40
problem-solving analyses, 75

FIGURES, USE OF
attention directing, 3, 24
factors affecting, 37
management's, 2, 22
problem solving, 3, 35
score card, 3, 24
FUNCTIONS
accounting, internal organization of, 66
accounting service, for sales, 90
common, in controller's department, 11
controllership, in surveyed companies, 11
differences, 12, 13
record keeping,
factories, 76
sales, 93
sales, accounting and control for, 89

GENERAL MILLS, INC.—FOOD DIV.
centralization, degree of, 19, 20
communications, 55
factory accounting executive, 17
organization, 40

105

A LONG-RANGE PROGRAM
OF RESEARCH IN CONTROLLERSHIP

The basic elements of a Long-Range Program for Research in Controllership are outlined on the following pages. This Program has been developed with reference to:

1. Recommendations of the Joint Committee on Long-Range Research Objectives.
2. Recommendations of the National Committee on Management Planning and Control.
3. Discussions with individual members of the Foundation Board of Trustees and its Executive Committee and of Controllers Institute.
4. Discussion of Foundation research at various meetings of Controls, national committees, and technical committees of the New York City Control.
5. The official Research Policy recently approved by the Foundation's Board of Trustees.

The wide diversity of interests of Institute members, their companies and those who make subscriptions/contributions to the Foundation is a factor considered in developing the Program. Finally, the Program is based on the premise that Foundation research must:

1. Make fundamental and lasting contributions to Controllership as an integral part of business management.
2. Study important specific actual or foreseeable developments of significance to controllers.

Those fundamental elements of the Program and its major topical divisions are outlined below. These divisions correspond to the basic functions of Controllership as officially defined by Controllers Institute. The Program is sufficiently broad in scope to serve as a long-range goal or plan of Foundation operations. It can be an effective guide for developing specific projects and maintaining adequate diversification of research operations.

THE PROGRAM

A. Basic Research on Concept, Techniques and Practice

I. *Controllership — General Concept, Requirements, Practice*

1. **The Controllership Function in Business.**
2. **Personnel Requirements for Controllership.**
3. **The Controller's Department — Organization, Personnel, Operation.**
4. **The Coordinating Role of Controllership — Relations with Other Executives and Departments.**
5. **Case Histories Covering More Than One Basic Function of Controllership.**

II. *Establishing, Coordinating, Maintaining an Integrated Plan for Control of Operations*

1. The Concept of Management Planning and Control.
2. Organization for, and Actual Management Planning and Control Practice.
3. Forecasting Business Conditions.
4. Setting Long-Range Goals.
5. Developing Intermediate Programs.
6. Budgetary Control.
7. Developing Standard Costs.
8. Planning and Controlling Capital Requirements and Expenditures.
9. Case History Studies of Management Planning and Control Problems, Practices.

III. *Measuring Performance Against Approved Operating Plans and Standards, and Reporting and Interpreting to Management Results of Operations*

1. Accounting Problems and Policy.
2. Organizing for Accounting and Reporting.
3. Systems and Records for Management Accounting.
4. Financial and Operating Reports.
5. Analysis, Interpretation and Application.
6. Integrating Accounting and Reports Policy and Operations with Needs of Management and Operating Departments.

IV. *Measuring and Reporting on the Validity of Objectives of the Business and the Effectiveness of Policies, Organization Structure and Procedures in Attaining Those Objectives*

1. Organization for, and Practice of, Analysis and Staff Consultation Functions.
2. Appraising and Reporting on Validity of Company Goals, Objectives.
3. Analysis of Company Organization, Policy, Procedures and Their Effectiveness for Reaching Objectives.
4. General Research and Fact-Finding Activities.
5. General Consulting, Advisory and Interdepartmental Activities.

V. *Reporting to Government Agencies and Supervision of Tax Matters*

1. Government Regulations, Reports and Reporting Requirements.
2. Taxes.
3. Government Procurement.
4. Relation of Points 1-3 to Other Controllership Functions, Company Planning and Control Activities.

VI. *Protection of the Assets of the Business*

1. Valuation Problems and Policy.
2. Accounting for Changes in Values.
3. Internal Controls.
4. Auditing.

5. Insurance Protection.
6. Relation to Company Policy, Goals, Plans, Budgets, Fiscal Requirements, Costs, Pricing, Profits.

B. The Controllership Function of Interpreting and Reporting on Developments Influencing Attainment of Business Objectives

I. Internal Developments of Significance to Controllers[1]

1. Technological Changes of Significance to Controllers.
2. Basic Developments in Company Organization, Administration, Procedures and Operations of Significance to Controllers.
3. Studies of the Controllership Problems Posed by Technological and Administrative Developments and the Actual or Suggested Solutions Developed by Controllers and Other Executives.

II. External Developments Influencing Controllers' Functions [2]

The Impact on the Controllers' Functions of Actual or Probable Changes in —
1. Business or Economic Conditions.
2. Political or Governmental "Climate" and Policy.
3. The Social Structure or Public Opinion and Attitudes.

Studies of the B category should be timely investigations of the problems posed for controllers by specific developments (or probable developments) and typical or representative reactions of controllers to such developments. For example, a series of such studies could be made of the problems posed for controllers by actual or prospective significant changes in price levels or levels of business activity. In the case of actual developments, such research would help to bring out various kinds of policies set up and action taken by controllers of different kinds of business.

Translating the Program into Action
Developing Specific Research Projects —
Cooperation with Controllers Institute

Most of the topical divisions and subdivisions outlined above are too wide in scope to be workable research projects *per se*. The program would be put into operation by developing specific projects to study various aspects of these topical subdivisions.

Continuing contact and exchange of ideas with Institute members, executives of companies supporting the Foundation, and the operating units of the Institute and Foundation should provide an index of Controllership functions and problems which are of special interest because of existing or developing internal or external conditions affecting business.

Specific projects will be developed in close cooperation with the Foundation's Executive Committee, national committees of Controllers Institute, technical com-

---

[1] To be confined to elements of the controller's responsibilities described in point 3 of the Institute's definition of Controllership.

[2] To be confined to elements of the controller's responsibilities described in point 5 of the Institute's definition of Controllership.

mittees of Local Controls and interested individual members of Controllers Institute. Such working relationships would involve discussing with appropriate groups or individuals ideas and suggestions for research projects, exploring various aspects of project problems, and cooperatively developing project proposals with adequate statement of scope and objectives.

Once such project proposals have been reviewed and approved by the Foundation's Executive Committee, working relations with the Institute should be maintained by establishing a project Advisory Panel made up of Institute members specially interested and competent in the particular project topic. Working in cooperation with the Foundation Research Director, the Panel would —

1. Consult with the Research Director and the project research team.
2. Periodically review progress and work of the research team with reference to project scope and objectives approved by the Executive Committee.
3. Review the research team's written report.
4. Appraise the report for possible publication by the Foundation and recommend appropriate action to the Foundation Executive Committee.